ENDORSEMENTS

I have always believed that one _____ ve
preparation. I'd like to say tha _____ ____ Tom to
come to the U of Iowa. The pre _____ _____ion and the hard
work on the mat are what brough___ ___in Ryan to campus, leaving
Syracuse and a full scholarship behind. The first day of practice
was a tough one for him. But Tom showed up more ready to
go on the second day and then the third and then the fourth.
Seeing this made me realize that Iowa wrestling had a potential
new wrestler who would fit in very well, and he did. In reality,
we got a little lucky, which doesn't happen often.

Dan Gable, Olympic Gold Medalist,
University of Iowa,
21-time Big Ten Champion Coach (consecutive),
16-time NCAA Championship coach

Coach Tom Ryan has been an inspiration to me and a
difference-maker to everyone who has the good fortune to be
in his company. He is always available for a call or text when
you need his faithful strength. I consider Tom Ryan to be an
authentic influencer in my life.

Jim Tressel, Head Football Coach,
The Ohio State University,
National Championship Coach 2012

Tom Ryan was a top-notch teammate who came to Iowa to learn
how to win the right way. He is open-minded and continues to
be better every day. Tom is a lifetime friend who has dealt with
life-shattering adversity, putting life skills to the real test. He is
a genuine, high-minded friend with selfless ambitions to make
everyone around him better.

Terry Brands, Associate Head Coach,
University of Iowa, Teammate,
Two-Time World Champion,
Olympic Bronze Medalist

Tom's willingness to put everything on the line earned him the respect of Hawkeye Nation when he came to Iowa. Tom's passion, desire, and drive are what set him apart from many others. He made a huge impact on everyone around him and was a large part of the success we had at Iowa in the early 1990s.

Troy Steiner, Head Coach Fresno State,
Iowa Teammate

I knew from the beginning that Tom Ryan was different. He had a certain spark within him. As we came into the Iowa Program, we had a lot of hopes and dreams. There is no doubt that his passion, drive, and energy was a great part of our individual and team success.

Terry Steiner, Head Women's Olympic Coach,
Iowa Teammate

Tom always had an edge. From kickball to football in the schoolyard, he never gave an inch. He always wanted to win. *Always*. It made you hate him or gravitate to him. When I started to lift with him in Jr High, it wasn't fun at first. He was a perfectionist. If you spotted him wrong or didn't work hard enough, you could see the disdain in his face or the frustration in his voice. And that's when you hated him. But weeks and months later, when you saw the results, you learned those infuriating things weren't to frustrate you but to make you better and want to follow him into the fire. That extra rep, the lunges up and down his inclined driveway, the run home from the gym after legs, the wrestling film all served to encourage you. He dragged this little Jewish kid to four weeks in Iowa, suffering through four practices a day. It all made you better and want to train. He gave me the mindset not that I could win, but I should expect to win.

I don't wonder why Tom has been so successful in his personal and wrestling life. If you're lucky enough to get pulled into his circle, you'd serve yourself well to embrace it.

Jon Adwar, High School Teammate

Tom and I came to Hofstra University at the same time, both first-time head coaches. We immediately developed a friendship based on our young families and respect for each other's relentless drive to build respected programs. We both took over struggling programs. We didn't have much financial support, but Tom had far less. I admired his love for his family, his passion, and his commitment. He never gave in to negativity, failure, or lack of support. He always persevered with a positive attitude that inspired his team and me.

I'm so proud of Tom's success and am not surprised at all. I'm more proud to call him a friend because of the husband, father, and mentor he has always been. His vision, work ethic, and positive attitude are inspirational to many today. But he's the same humble, hard-working, good man he's always been. Success has not affected him. I admire his humility and continued drive to make his wrestlers the best version of themselves.

Jay Wright, Villanova Men's Basketball Coach,
Two-Time National Championship

I first met Coach Tom Ryan at an Athletes in Action event—a campus ministry for student-athletes at Ohio State. We soon became friends. We share a common intensity and focus on our faith, our family, and our team. I became a fan of wrestling, more so a fan of Coach Ryan and his team. Rather quickly I saw that his players shared his values of faith, family, and team. The football team won the 2014 National Championship, and Coach Ryan and his team soon followed with the 2015 National Championship.

His story of tragic loss and searching for the answers were so compelling that I've asked him to speak to my team on several occasions. His story is one of love and testimony.

Urban Meyer, Assistant Athletic Director,
The Ohio State University,
Former Ohio State University Football Coach

I could not have asked for a better person, teammate, and brother to have experienced all that comes from life and its dramatic twists and turns, highs and lows. As boys and young men, competition was the constant in our lives. It didn't matter if it was kickball in the street, running bases with our extended family at our grandparent's house, a home run derby at our local elementary school, darts, or wrestling in high school and college, we were battling for the win. The lessons we took from those events, especially those we learned in wrestling, taught us how to challenge ourselves and sacrifice and gain from suffering. Ultimately, pursuing wrestling the way we did undoubtedly enabled us to manage life more effectively and overcome the most overwhelmingly challenging times and darkest periods. Pondering all of this as a 52-year-old man, I feel an immense sense of gratitude and thanks.

Frank Ryan, 2-time Syracuse Team Captain,
Syracuse Law School,
President DLA Piper Law Firm

There is nothing like what it takes to excel in the sport of wrestling. Natural ability won't get you very far at all. It's all about who's willing to do the things, go the places, and sacrifice more for the chance to become great. Dreams don't last long in wrestling; only a passion for hunting and grinding will last long enough to get you to the top in this sport! Chosen suffering is a choice you must make to have any success, especially in wrestling. I love wrestling, and it's the one thing that has had the greatest impact on my life and made me who I am today.

Luke Fickell, Head Football Coach,
University of Cincinnati,
3-Time State Champ Wrestler
Started *every* Ohio State football game for four years

I'll never forget the first time Coach Tom shared his story with me and I heard him say these words: "God never wastes suffering." He is a living example of how to use one's life to glorify God and inspire others. I consider our friendship one of the greatest blessings of my life and having he, Lynette, and the kids join us in the mission of Rock City Church has been a tremendous gift.

Chad Fisher, Pastor, Rock City Church

CHOSEN SUFFERING

Becoming Elite in Life and Leadership

TOM RYAN

Head Coach of The Ohio State University
National Championship Wrestling Team

with Kirsten D Samuel

⟆AUTHOR
ACADEMY elite

Published by Author Academy Elite
P.O. Box 43, Powell, OH 43065
www. AuthorAcademyElite.com

Library of Congress Cataloging: 2019913946
Softcover: 978-1-64085-917-3
Hardcover: 978-1-64085-918-0
E-book: 978-1-64085-919-7

Available in hardcover, softcover, e-book, and audiobook

Dedication

To all of those who have suffered, paused,
pursued wisdom diligently, surrendered to a lasting truth,
and changed direction.

TABLE OF CONTENTS

FOREWORD

My life could be separated into two distinct eras. The first phase was my life *before* Jesus; the second is my life *after* Jesus. The first period was marked by a self-centered, narcissistic lifestyle mired in hopelessness and ignorance. The later era has been marked by grace, hope, and unconditional surrender to the One who died so we could be reconciled forever.

As a man healed by Jesus said in John 9:25, "One thing I do know. I was blind but now I see!"

Maybe that sounds dramatic, but it's real—and stories like mine are more common than you may think. Everyone starts out in phase one, but unfortunately not everyone experiences phase two. Those who do often find it hard to explain to others the night-and-day difference they've enjoyed because of their encounter with the living God.

If you don't know my story, I am an atheist-turned-Christian, the former award-winning legal editor of *The Chicago Tribune,* and best-selling author of more than forty books and curricula.

I spent the earlier part of my career convinced God doesn't exist. Ultimately, Truth won me over. Faced with the facts of science and history, I had nowhere to go except to my knees.

No two spiritual journeys are alike, which is what makes all of them so fascinating. The destination may be the same, but the route to God can take a variety of different paths. For my friend Tom Ryan, it was a trail of suffering.

Like many of us, Tom's life was uneventful—until it wasn't any longer. I don't wish his loss on anyone. Through it all, his pain could have made him bitter or better. It did neither, at least in the beginning.

This suffering broke Tom, his pride, and his self-reliance. When he found the end of himself, he finally found the beginning of God.

It reminds me of A.W. Tozer's words: "God cannot use a man or woman greatly until He wounds them deeply." One thing is for sure: You won't find those words on a Hallmark card. They're not nice, neat, or sanitized. Instead, they're raw, relatable—and true. Suffering isn't some cruel punishment poured out by an angry God. Rather, it's a tool used by a loving Father to set us free.

The book you're about to read isn't easy. Quite the opposite. It's messy. After all, why would anyone choose suffering? Well, you're about to find out. Maybe the path toward victory is paved with suffering—at least, it was for the One who carried His cross on the road to Calvary.

Tom's book might transform the way you see yourself and the God who made you. It's quite fitting he shares it against the backdrop of wrestling. This metaphor fits the adventure you're about to take.

You'll wrestle yourself. You'll wrestle truth. And you'll wrestle God. Just ask Jacob from the Bible. He wrestled with God and it changed him forever—literally and figuratively. He would walk with a limp for the rest of his life. But he *Lee Strobel and Tom Ryan.*

would also walk closer to God. If you could ask him, he'd tell you it was all worth the suffering.

It's been said that you should never trust a leader without a limp. Tom Ryan is a leader who walks with such a limp. He knows suffering, and it has shaped him to become victorious in life and leadership. Tom's life could be divided into two eras too. Phase one was life *before* Jesus; phase two is life *after* Jesus. In one phase he was dead; in the other, he was reborn. One was defined by *unchosen* suffering; the other by *chosen* suffering. Read on and you'll soon discover the difference between the two. And trust me—his story will mark your life. Just remember that as you walk this path, you're not alone. As Tom learned, God will never leave you or forsake you.

Lee Strobel
New York Times best-selling author
Director of The Strobel Center at Colorado Christian University

PREFACE
THE 3 SUCCESS PILLARS

There's an empty space in every human being that longs to be filled. The world provides an array of possibilities and options we hope will fill that void.

For thirty-six years, I tried to make wrestling and many other things fill that space. None of these could, no matter how hard I tried. Only one thing can. The question isn't how we fill that space, but more importantly, the long term effects the filling agent has on our life. In essence, is the space-filling material able to sustain us for the long haul, or is it fool's gold that offers a euphoric feeling incapable of lasting?

Those who have experienced sustained success have left us all clues, which we'll explore more in-depth. Every person wants to pursue excellence and chase big dreams while simultaneously experiencing contentment and tranquility. Some get side-tracked while some go off the tracks.

There's no perfect life, and our best life doesn't happen by chance—nothing does. We need to understand there are principles to becoming Elite. The more frequently we apply these principles, the better we increase the odds of living our best life. I call these the 3 Success Pillars, which I'll list now and expound upon later.

Pillar #1: Your mind. This is the internal you, where all your thoughts originate.

Pillar #2: Your relationships. This is who you allow to influence your decisions.

Pillar #3: Your environment. This is the setting that will build you or break you.

The world doesn't care what we're after, nor does it care about *our* principles. It doesn't care about you or me, nor will it change for us. It doesn't owe us anything. The world is heading in a direction—spinning on its axis, and there's little we can do to change that. What we can change, however, is what we do. We can control our direction.

> YOU'LL NEVER CHANGE YOUR LIFE UNTIL YOU CHANGE SOMETHING YOU DO DAILY. THE SECRET OF YOUR SUCCESS WILL BE FOUND IN YOUR DAILY ROUTINE.
>
> JOHN MAXWELL

We must continuously develop our *core* and *worldview* to help us navigate the temptations of the world. On the journey to find our purpose, we must set boundaries on what we will tolerate and won't.

This all starts with our minds—what we bring into it and extract from it. This is the battleground that must be won hour after hour, day after day, week after week. It's a never-ending fight. The six-inch space between our ears must remain vigilant to war daily.

No one can lead until they can lead themselves. Start simple. Wake up on time. Make your bed. Put away your dishes. Keep your room clean. Build simple habits. Repair *you*. Stop lying to yourself and others. Share the truth. Build yourself into someone strong. Only then will others look your way.

Do something uncomfortable, but right. Apologize to someone you wronged. Bounce your truth off reality, not your own truth. Be real even when it's not popular. Stop playing the part of a yes man or a yes woman.

When our words are clean, honest, and fair, no matter what happens in the moment, it's going to be for good. You will grow to like yourself more, which is great because that's who you'll be spending the most time with.

We must develop a strong and deeply rooted worldview set in solid principles. If not, we should prepare to lose our shallow roots and be tossed back-and-forth. We're never far from a positive transformation in our lives.

Can you imagine your child, neighbor, brother, cousin, or friend valuing the opinions of social media so much they feel deplcted and take their life? I could write for days on the topic. Chasing the love of likes, retweets, and comments is dangerous when they become a principle by which we value ourselves. The human mind is precious, and like James Allen points out, it must be cultivated.[1]

> *A man's mind be likened to a Garden, which may be intelligently cultivated or allowed to run wild; but whether cultivated or neglected it must and will bring forth. If no useful seeds are put into it, then an abundance of useless weed seeds will fall therein, and will continue to produce their kind.*

What we allow in our mind must be well-vetted because, over time, it's reflected in our actions. Our daily choices mirror our thoughts. It's our birthright to block and evict negative thoughts that don't belong and welcome life-giving thoughts into our minds. This is hard. But, anything worth attaining is.

The first step is to make sure we understand this truth and pursue it. We must fight to reclaim our headspace.

The second step is to understand where the fountain of timeless principles can be found. Drinking dirty water can be harmful. Therefore, we must drink from the life-giving well. I discovered this well at thirty-six-years old. Deep suffering caused me to search for it. If we don't know what we're looking for and where we can find it, we end up searching aimlessly for years. The world won't provide such principles as it only offers what's relevant at the moment, and its water is often dirty. Simply put, the world wants us to feel good. It'll send us off track and mislead us at every corner. The world wants to soften our minds and to chase the easy way and whatever feels good. We're the landlord of our minds, and we must work diligently to maintain its beauty.

The truth is, more people absorb this mentality than don't. Most never attach their existence to their purpose. They have no road map and wander aimlessly through life, choosing the path of least resistance. Our desire to get uncomfortable and suffer is at an all-time low.

Chosen suffering is a mindset and action that should be a foundational ingredient embedded in our lives. The world says lay on the couch, eat chips, avoid tough conversations, and be comfortable. The timeless principles of the Elite say the opposite. We get to choose, but the daily application of this principle is hard.

There are various ways our minds can be affected:

- The people we surround ourselves with

- The environments we are in

- The source of our wisdom

What we learn in our home, schools, peer groups, communities, television, chat rooms, social media, and music integrate into our thought life and ultimately become determiners in how high we climb.

These factors guide us as they become part of our view of this world.

These choices are literally life or death. Let's start with the people we surround ourselves with and then explore environments. Why do we choose the people we do? If we believe people matter, we should be very deliberate about who we allow into our inner circle and why we allow them in. I'm not saying to be judgmental and turn away from people and not offer love to them. There are few things unhealthier than judging those around us.

What I'm saying is the right people matter as they impact our underlining values. As a leader of two different Division I programs and the father of four, I'm cognizant of this timeless principle. The right people in my life are a significant reason why I am where I am. I have hired the best assistant coaches and surrounded myself with great leaders. If my children or anyone I love were around the wrong people, I'd stop it. I'd execute all measures within the law to see that mind-polluting relationships are moved away from anyone I love.

We must be willing to let people go who are a virus to our mindset or a deterrent to an organization. This is challenging as we can get caught up trying to change them.

As a coach, I have a long leash, and sometimes I should let people go sooner than I do. The age-old principle is to be slow to hire and quick to fire. Struggle reveals who people are. Once it does, take immediate assessment and action. Either they're building us up or breaking us down. There's no in-between. They're either giving to or taking from others. Make the distinction then make the decision.

As a parent, it's our earthly responsibility to know timeless principles and ensure our children understand each of them and have the courage to apply them. Application is always the toughest component to any plan.

Jack Miller, a friend from Wooster, Ohio, who elevates my thought life, shared a story about some prison ministry work. When he asked the inmates what they believed caused them to be where they are, nearly all of them said, "I just started hanging out with this one guy. He introduced me to the wrong crowd."

We must be deliberate about the friendship choices we make. The men I've coached who excelled at the highest level all followed this principle. I counted on every one of them because they were reliable.

Even when I choose to walk my dogs, I'm intentional about who I walk with. We have plenty of neighbors, but my choice is a life-giving friend, Phil Anglim. We talk about uplifting things, challenge each other, and help keep our core strong. Negative conversation takes life and wastes our energy.

I also have two mentors who help me gain clarity when the world seeps in. Tom Rode, a great friend, leads a group called Cross Sports on campus for student-athletes and coaches. He fills me with wisdom and clear thinking. Another mentor is Chet Scott, who runs an organization called Built to Lead. He meets with me and my team. Both men share truth in love with me. I need this. We all need this. I've remained friends with many uplifting men who've helped me when I was coaching at Hofstra as well.

All my life, I've gravitated toward uplifting people and handpicked those who love others and want to serve. I look for men of high character, and I choose to recruit and hire this trait above their expertise in wrestling. Character is a sustainable force that builds culture.

> CHARACTER IS A SUSTAINABLE FORCE THAT BUILDS CULTURE.

People are the key ingredient in any culture. Based on their worldview, they push and pull us either forward or backward and lift us, but not always. They bring good and bad and force us to navigate their words and actions. More often than not, we choose the people in our lives. We should know them well.

We must consider what source we plug our energy cord into. Our thoughts matter. This truth follows us throughout every stage and season of our lives. Study any human, and you'll find a direct correlation between their thought life and level or lack of success. Our thoughts are the control tower that navigates the people and the environments we pursue.

Environments and their cultures have a great effect on us. As parents, we battle to ensure our children choose the right friends, attend the right schools, attend a youth group, worship at church, get involved with the best sports clubs, learn from the best coaches, and get embedded into the toughest environments.

It seems so simple, but it's not. Many don't have the opportunity for any of this. Life is about survival for some. Many are beaten down and disappointed, and there aren't positive or powerful examples, so the negative or wrong things are elevated. In turn, deeper issues are never explored or discussed. Opportunity is rarely equal.

For those with opportunity, they sometimes move toward the easy way and fool's gold. It's hard to manage so much, so many don't. Our will and temptation pull us off course, and we allow feelings rather than facts to guide us. The world is filled with varying scenarios. We all fight its nasty grip. It promises us a false sense of having things now and encourages us to pursue instant gratification, but often attacks when we're emotionally experiencing hard things.

Movies span around ninety minutes, highlighting the here to there as though that's enough time to showcase the true struggle that's foundational in growth. Infomercials advocate perfect abs in ten minutes. The quick-fixes are untrue and deceitful to our psyche. It's a lie. It preloads inaccuracies that lead us to not being ready for the agony it takes to grow and flourish.

The iPhone offers us immediate feedback. Technology is a blessing and a curse. We don't have to wait for anything anymore. We can have it now, and we often want it now. We can pay extra for next day delivery.

Pain is a must, and it's best not to go through it alone. Our desires must be stronger than any barrier which stands between us and them. This is especially true because barriers

> BY YOURSELF YOU'RE
> UNPROTECTED.
> WITH A FRIEND YOU
> CAN FACE THE WORST.
> ECCLESIASTES 4:12
> THE MESSAGE

are ever-changing and elusive. A creative, solution-based mindset is so important because it helps us develop small, life-changing habits.

We'll always be the sum total of the people who lifted us or weighed us down along the journey and the environments we chose.

I've learned that Chosen Suffering is a must. Chosen and unchosen suffering have offered me the deepest life lessons. This is a story about love and sacrifice, heartache and pain, trust and wisdom, competence and connection. But ultimately, this story is about the piercing effect the death of my beloved son, Teague, had on me and how it led me to my faith. I hope it inspires you, causes you to pursue wisdom, commit to the tougher things, and transform into more.

Tom Ryan
Head Coach
The Ohio State Wrestling Team

INTRODUCTION
THE COLLISION OF
TWO SUFFERINGS

*God whispers to us in our pleasures, speaks in our conscience,
but shouts in our pains: it is his megaphone
to rouse a deaf world.*

—CS Lewis

"The 2015 NCAA Wrestling Team Championship Title goes to The Ohio State University! Their first-ever wrestling team title," said the ESPN analyst.

Though Ohio State University has fielded a wrestling team since 1920, finally, after ninety-five years, the Buckeye Nation raised a National Championship in one of the state's most deep-rooted sports.

Euphoric emotions overflowed as the last twenty-three years of hard work, dreams, and discipline all came to fruition on this evening. Fans, donors, fellow coaches, and athletes erupted with happiness. From the competition floor, I looked up toward my family, seated in the arena. My wife, our three children, my brother, sister, nephews, and parents were filled with happiness, but now wasn't the time to celebrate with them.

As my phone flooded with congratulatory messages, one struck my soul hard. A true, long-time friend during the most difficult challenge in my life, Billy Baldwin, said in a text to my wife, "How elated Teague must be for his Dad." It shot agonizing pain through my heart. Billy knew my pain.

Two types of suffering collided in that moment.

Upon reading my wife's text containing Billy's comment, I quickly moved to a quiet corner under the arena seats, out of sight of the 20,000 roaring fans and athletes that filled the underbody of the arena, and dropped to my knees behind a dark curtain.

Searing, gut-wrenching tears burst from the depths of my soul—the pain of indescribable loss, unfulfilled potential, and erased dreams stung. It felt like I was drowning again.

Time had taught me a new normal, but it never completely healed the wounds. Scars healed but remained tender. Even though eleven years had passed since his death, it's not enough time to heal deep loss.

How is it that pain stirs us more than success? Why does a human experience this type of pain? What good can it produce?

How could I, in this pinnacle moment of my career and dreams, be both ecstatic and crushed?

CS Lewis wrestled with this question in his book, *The Problem of Pain*. As Lewis discovered, pain heightens our senses, highlighting every facet of life with HD clarity. In this summit moment of my career, which resulted in extreme happiness, another life-track ran concurrently—the most profound personal grief. Time had passed, but never completely healed the gaping wound.

I lived in the intersection between two sufferings—chosen and unchosen. Every emotion achingly defined and heightened to inscribe the moment indelibly on my heart and mind.

I understood and longed for chosen suffering because its roots were deeply embedded in my life and the life of every Elite performer I'd ever met. Chosen suffering is a foundation to growth and is non-negotiable for progress. It's a timeless truth. The more, the better. It's caused by the choices we make—good and bad. Chosen suffering by so many led us to this National title.

However, unchosen suffering is different. It's the force of nature pressing down on our lives. It's the ever-present reminder that we're here to manage the painful things we didn't cause but happen to us and those we love. Unchosen sufferings come at various times, in varying shapes and sizes and levels. Sufferings don't discriminate but can educate through the hurt. All require a deep yearning to find the meaning even when one doesn't seem to be in our view. Unchosen suffering transformed me in a different way. It exposed a blind spot and created a deep yearning to inspect my vision of this life.

While experiencing the gifts from sustained hard work over time, the deepest grief overwhelmed me. Chosen and unchosen suffering were side-by-side.

This evening, I was aware that extreme pain and happiness could live alongside each other. In the human condition, each person walks these tracks and faces the two forces. The emotional struggle lasted for a few intense minutes. Billy's words instantly took me to a season of total devastation. Alone with Teague in that quiet space, I ached.

It was then time to celebrate with the men whose chosen suffering led us to this NCAA Team Title. They set the standard for all other Ohio State wrestling teams to follow.

I wiped my tears and walked through that dark curtain.

2015 NCAA Championship. The Ohio State's first ever wrestling title acknowledging the timeless gifts of chosen suffering.

Chapter 1
Positive Infinity

Positive infinity crashes
any pity party

The soul which has no fixed purpose in life is lost;
to be everywhere is to be nowhere.

—Michael de Montaigne

Everyone was created *on* purpose and *for* a purpose. The journey is to find and foster it.

Chosen suffering has guided me, helped me progress, left me empty at times, yet it was unchosen suffering that destroyed me, and transformed me.

When you feel like you are unsatisfied or when you're suffering, pay attention to this important sign. How we manage this suffering is what matters the most. It's not necessarily a sign that you need to do more, although it could. It doesn't necessarily mean you need to work harder, but you might. It certainly doesn't mean you need to pursue happiness through objects like financial status, more trophies, fancier cars, or winning more. Sometimes, it's a sign that what we are pursuing and seeking at a fundamental level is not attainable in our current lives.

When you are in the midst of suffering—no matter the degree—it should disrupt your typical process. It should awaken you to the truth in the ultimate sense you cannot be satisfied with your current state of mind and daily existence. In essence, something needs to change. Likely, it is the thing on which you lean to bring you peace.

In my life, until unchosen suffering surfaced, I looked inside myself to find the answers. Although introspection is critical, it can't stop there. There is a more powerful truth. The world offers many options that lead nowhere. Your suffering should move you to reorient your approach to the game of life. It should push you to something larger and greater than yourself. It should give you awe, silence, and peace. Suffering needs to be difficult and painful for you to seek something beyond it and beyond you.

Unchosen suffering led me to this place. It took me to the deepest hurt I have ever felt, and I responded to it. I pursued wisdom, encountered truth, and surrendered to it. I began to build my life around this truth. There was an incredible healing power that occurred, which I will unpack in the chapters to come.

Suffering is a sign that calls us to transform our actions through a change in not only *thinking* about changing while engaging in old, unhelpful habits. You must take meaningful action to transform your life and transcend old habits that bind you and create your suffering. My transformation required full ownership and, of course, spiritual practices.

Ultimately, you must take responsibility for your state of mind. You must grab the wheel and change your destination. You might even need to hand the wheel to something greater. Yes, we all suffer. But the most important part of suffering is deciding how you will respond to its inevitable influence on your life. If we do not, it is wasted suffering.

I was fortunate to be gifted with special parents and grow up in a middle-class town surrounded by many eager people who wanted to live their best life. Sure, it wasn't perfect, but I was lifted so many times. I've lived in a world that rewarded hard work and success. The wrestling room is a special place. There's no hiding in a one-to-one competition. Every high-level wrestler or successful leader I've had the privilege of interacting with applied these principles, and that led them to the success they've earned. They all choose to suffer. They have great emotional control and understand aggression's relationship to progress.

Growing up on Long Island, New York, our family worked hard. Each person had a role to play to sustain our family. My parents taught us you can do anything if you work hard enough. I had endless energy as a kid and was always eager for more. My energy level was far closer to that of a marathon runner than a couch potato. We all fall somewhere between the two.

As an avid entrepreneur, Dad owned a restaurant and worked long, hard hours. Mom worked as a waitress but still managed our home well. In our family, we didn't discuss finances. We always had enough. At least that was my perception as a young pre-teenager. Sure, some of my friends had things I didn't have, but I never felt deprived because we didn't want for anything.

I never assessed myself on what we had or didn't have because my parents never did. Nor did anyone around me. Our family had everything that mattered—community, love, belief, honesty, trust, stability, commitment, and acceptance—but the greatest one was love. We all felt loved. It's hard to imagine a life without these things as a foundation. Yet, so many don't have this foundation. Somehow they overcome the toughest childhoods where so much suffering occurred.

They use the suffering for good in their lives. It transforms them into something greater. They rise above it, and they don't waste their suffering.

My journey to understand what I call chosen and unchosen suffering began with the separation of my parents. At the time, my underdeveloped mind couldn't define what was happening. Suffering isn't something I would've referred to as a foundational piece of growth back then. These terms are the result of my life's reflection and the enlightening perspective that suffering and quiet reflection can provide. It was a tough time for my parents and my two siblings. My parents simply couldn't get along, so in the end, their separation was best.

Dad and Mom divorced around my first-grade year. High school sweethearts, they were married with three children by the age of twenty-one. They took on so much at a young age, which is hard to manage. Eventually, the four of us moved in with my grandparents, who were a real gift. We all shared one of the two upstairs bedrooms for the next two years. My great-grandmother lived in the bedroom across the hall—three generations living in the same home who took care of each other. I never remember feeling deprived because of the compact space. As I reflect, I suppose that's because more room doesn't equate to a deeper connection. Lots of big houses are filled with empty hearts. We loved it because we were together. Size is only relative to the connections of each person.

Nanny & PopPop's House

My dad lived in Atlanta, GA, and I missed him. There were no FaceTime, Zoom calls, or cell phones during those years, but he often called and wrote. I remember how hard it was

4

to read his letters. He also attended nearly all of the critical dates in our life. Anyone who's been through a separation knows the evenly dispersed pain in it for everyone. I knew my mom and dad were in pain. We learned at a young age to focus forward and find the gifts in each day. We concentrated on what we had instead of what we didn't. I truly thank my parents for that.

The other reality is that kids are resilient. No child lives in the perfect setting because it doesn't exist. You find your power by pulling the blessings away from any environment rather than the negatives.

The human mind needs to be harnessed. We have so many thoughts and choices on a given day. Excuses and blame long to root themselves in our lives as much as accountability and ownership. We choose which to feed and grow. The starved one will weaken. It helped that Mom and Dad never spoke poorly of each other, which is a powerful lesson for me to this day. Negativity doesn't produce growth, which is something I never experienced growing up. I never heard my mom or dad talk bad about neighbors, teachers, or anyone else.

With my father living in a different state, I was fortunate to have several men in my life who were there for the day-to-day events that helped me grow. Always at my grandparents' home, Uncle Tony took an interest in me and my wrestling career. He was both fun and funny. Uncle Tony made a big deal out of little things, and I liked that. If I won a local junior high tournament, he would beep the horn all the way home. He made me feel special. Uncle Tony's two daughters, my cousins Mary and Ann Marie, were special women. He would often tell me I was the son he never had. I had a tremendous support network and am thankful for it.

My nanny and pop-pop, Eleanor and Anthony, were the real deal. They took the four of us into their home when we needed them. As the son of Italian immigrants, Pop-Pop worked hard for the town and loved America and what it offered him. Nanny took care of everyone by cooking excellent tasting Italian food. Her meatballs and marinara sauce were a taste of heaven. Nanny wore the shirt, "Always right," and Pop-Pop's shirt read, "Always wrong." I suppose that's why their marriage lasted until he passed. He learned marriage is designed for our holiness more so than our happiness.

My pop-pop was tough. He was a two-time golden glove champion, so fighting was in his DNA. He meant so much to us and gave more than we could repay—a place to stay, his time, guidance, example, and love. He cared for us, and I could feel it. I remember my nanny yelling at him for driving miles out of his way to save five cents on a loaf of bread. Because he understood what it was like to have little, not much was wasted in my grandparents' home.

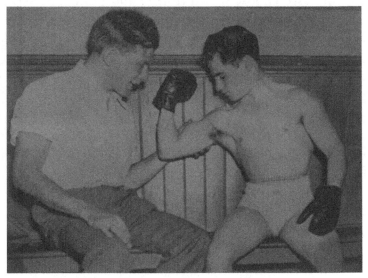

PopPop. Two-time Golden Glove champion. Circa 1936.

Nanny and Pop-Pop were always there for me and my siblings, Frank and Kim. Pop-Pop brought me to various wrestling camps and clinics and helped in any way he could. We attended camps all over Long Island, so without someone willing to sacrifice for us, we would have struggled to progress. He provided support whenever we needed it.

Pop-Pop taught us many lessons. Nanny did too. They mostly came at the dinner table. One night, the conversation got serious when my older brother, Frank, shared that the kid up the block was mouthing off and bullying him. As soon as Pop-Pop heard that, he stood up and told Frank to get his shoes on. "We're going to see that bully."

Although I was young, I went along because he was my brother. We all walked up the street and knocked on the bully's door. His dad answered, and Pop-Pop told him the situation. He said, "Your son needs to come out to the front lawn."

As a small second-grader freaked out but excited, I couldn't believe my eyes. The bully came out, and he and my brother squared off. All I remember of the fight was that it ended quickly. I walked back to our house with a puffed-out chest. My brother stopped the street bully's reign. I must admit I loved it. Five years later, I learned about the sport of wrestling. Though I don't condone fighting, I do advocate facing your problems head-on.

Every event in our lives reinforces a mindset, a creed to live by. So many spend their entire lives not knowing who they are, why they're here, and what to stand for. On this day, I learned many things. But the one that stood out the most was to fight for what I believe in. Winning mattered a whole bunch.

Mom worked hard to care for my siblings and me to the point I never felt neglected or deprived. Like many people, Mom was simple and yearned for consistency and stability.

Eventually, she remarried a wonderful guy named Sal Curiale, who had four children (Deb, Sue, Rob, and Chris). We were the Brady Bunch plus one. There were seven of us—two in second grade, two in third grade, two in fifth grade, and the oldest was in seventh grade. I was the middle—middle child in my family and middle in my blended family. Contrary to most theories, though, I didn't get lost or feel left out. How Mom and Sal, my step-dad, blended our two families amazes me to this day.

Mom, Rosalie, and Step-dad, Sal's, wedding. Top Row from Left to Right: Sue, Deb, Mom, Dad. Bottom row from left to right: Rob, Chris, Frank, Tom, Kim

We moved from my grandparents' house to Sal's house about two hundred yards away, roughly ten houses. We were fortunate she met someone who was an honest, hard-working man and lived so close to my grandparents. The neighborhood was filled with many who provided strong relationships for me.

My step-brother, Rob, was a good wrestler as well. We were the same age, and it was really fun watching him develop. He had a huge heart and loved the sport. As I reflect on his career, he didn't have the same opportunities that I had—the same house, but different opportunities. The love for him wasn't less, but, rather, with seven kids, Mom and Pop Sal couldn't afford to send Rob to the best camps. My father helped me and my brother Frank attend camps. I am fortunate to have had such opportunities granted to me. They changed my life.

Accepting opportunities that come mattered, and I welcomed them. I wanted more for my life and chosen suffering through physical training was the track I rode.

I'm grateful to Pop Sal for many things, but mostly for how much respect and love he showed my mom. She meant the world to him and us. They're still happily married, and she still holds the highest place in his heart. When I think about the sacrifices she made for us, it's hard not to feel grateful. Sal took care of our most treasured gift—Mom.

From my earliest years, I learned the value of hard work. As the rock of our family, Mom worked long hours to pay for groceries (not something I knew as a child). She always had a home-cooked meal ready for our family of nine. Every night, we ate dinner together at our dining room table, a picnic table with a beautiful covering. Mom was amazing, and one of her gifts was cooking good food. Her mom taught her. That's how Italians do things. I don't remember ever going out for dinner during my entire childhood while with Mom and Sal. Not once. Mom worked, cooked, cleaned, and gave. Pop Sal did too.

In our home, we talked a whole bunch about anything and everything. And we laughed together. These face-to-face communication skills prepared me to play my part in the world. You had to know who you were and what role you played in the family. Everyone was integral to our family's success, which taught me the importance of community.

Holidays, birthdays, and special events were so much fun. We played cards, board games, and laughed. I loved to win

The Long Island house the nine of us lived in.

and hated to lose. Games were always competitive—no mercy, no looking back. I lived in somewhat of a bubble of pure love, few distractions, no internet, cell phones, or social media. We had each other. Of course, there was some fighting here and there, but that wasn't the essence of our home.

> THERE IS LITTLE SUCCESS WHERE THERE IS LITTLE LAUGHTER.
>
> ANDREW CARNEGIE

Too many times, we neglect the importance of building a robust and healthy community. Each person needs support and encouragement. My family overflowed with this kind of community. Laughter filled our home. Seven children shared three bedrooms. My three sisters lived in the biggest room, and the four of us brothers shared two rooms.

Having two dads could've been a problem, but not in my case. My father, Frank, had big guts. He wasn't afraid to work relentlessly and take chances. He was incredibly uplifting and taught me to believe in myself. Dad and Pop Sal supported me, participated in my life, and believed in me. My parents gave me the single greatest gift you can give anyone—belief. I never heard negative critiques when I tried something new. Instead, Dad, Mom, and Pop Sal believed and encouraged me to work hard, give it my best, and see what happened. They were busy running their lives; they left mine up to me. I liked it that way.

My dad earned success in the restaurant business, working long hours to provide for us. But as I reflect, I realize how many opportunities he helped me with to get me where I am today. He supported my desire to attend the most challenging camps and financially helped me attend the University of Iowa. Dad provided us with opportunities that needed resources. Becoming a high-level wrestler or Elite athlete in any sport has a cost. But he also enabled me with much more. He taught me to dream big and to chase with a relentless heart. He showed me what fearless looked like. He was kind of like

Yoda, "Train yourself to let go of everything you fear to lose." This mindset was so valuable for me and would show up over and over in my life.

Every summer my two siblings and I went to Atlanta, Georgia. In the divorce, Mom got us during the school year and Dad had us for the summers. Atlanta was hot but fun. There was a community pool and a full-service fitness center. That's all we needed. We would compete then cool down. Summers with Dad were special.

Mom and Sal weren't able to help with the finances. My dad was, and each of my parents offered what they could, which was what I needed. My childhood wasn't perfect, but it certainly provided me with some of the intangibles required to build a life around. I realize now, that deep unchosen suffering didn't play a role in my life as a kid, but it would eventually.

The town of Wantagh, just thirty-five miles west of New York City and seven miles north of the Atlantic Ocean, teemed with community. My block alone had several kids who went on to earn D1 scholarships. They were all my friends. All were runners and wrestlers—fast, focused, and tough. They all understood chosen suffering. They were the type of friends every parent wants their kids around. One classmate, Mike Hedgecock, lived directly across the street. We often dreamed of running a big charter fishing boat together down south. He ran a 4:10 mile in high school, and his dad, one of our high school cross county coaches, was one of the nation's best. I was blessed to have Mike as a friend and his dad as a coach. Mike went to the University of South Carolina and broke some records there.

Tom Ryan, Gerard Castro, Mike Hedgecock.
Growing up around competitive people was a blessings.
Both Gerard and Mike went on to run in college.

Around the block was Jerry Castro. He and Dave Levin attended Kent State on track and cross-country scholarships. Jerry is now one of the best high school cross country coaches in America. His passion transformed the development of runners in a small community in North Carolina. He understands the sport and the deeper purpose of life. He built a big following, and people move toward him. I often call him to discuss training plans for my Ohio State team. Coach Bill Hedgecock, Mike's father, saw me running all the time for wrestling and finally convinced me to run cross country. I'm glad I did. Running with people faster than me was important. These guys really pushed me. On our runs, they extended my discomfort threshold. When I was hurting, they weren't hurting nearly as much. Coach Hedgecock made me understand running, and years later, it helped me to become a better coach. I learned a valuable mindset lesson that running was far more about one's mind than legs. I'm a big believer in the positive effects of running for wrestling and a better life.

My friends and I competed at everything. Mix in an older brother and two step-brothers and a large grass field around the corner, and we had the ingredients for great competitions. Everyday life consisted of competing. I nurtured the gift of my circle of friends. Winning mattered.

From second grade to ninth grade, I played traditional sports—baseball, soccer, track, and basketball. I liked them all, but basketball was my favorite. My life revolved around sports and being outdoors. I was never inside. There was no reason to be. Basketball was my first love, followed by soccer. Baseball was a bit slow, and I wasn't a very good hitter. I realize now that I didn't practice enough. The eye-hand coordination to hit a ball requires hard work. Barry Bonds, one of MLB's best hitters, hit often. He mastered his skill with focused practice. He was only allowed to swing at the odd-numbered golf balls his father tossed his way. He trained his eyes through repetition to see the spin on the golf ball and read the odd number. Simple. Brilliant. Hard work.

At a young age, I learned I hated losing more than I enjoyed winning. Anyone on my team was going to play hard or, well, I'd yell. I was a bit aggressive, and even as a young kid organizing pick-up games at the Forest Lake Elementary school field, I admired effort and expected it from anyone on my team. Playing for fun was good, but we always kept score. That means some people left winners and others losers. I might've rubbed victory in the face of my friends a bit too much. I only did it to be sure they'd come ready to play hard every time. I'm not certain I could trace this mindset back to anything in particular, but it was the one I adopted early on.

Throughout my elementary years, I averaged about ten points every basketball game. I liked having the ball. In life, some want the ball, and some don't. Some run toward it and some away. I was fairly disciplined and consistent like my parents taught me—hard work produces success. Something burned in me to always give my best. Basketball and other sports taught me to focus. I looked forward to competing for years to come.

In the seventh grade, when I tried out for the junior high basketball team, I experienced my first setback. All the elementary schools in our area feed into the junior high school. Naturally, the competition and stakes heightened. Leaning on my work ethic, I tried out for the team, confident in my skills.

Imagine my surprise when the morning after the three-day tryouts, I checked the team roster hanging on the locker room bulletin board only to see—nothing. My name wasn't there. I was convinced there was a mistake and found Coach O'Leary.

"Hey, Coach. My name's missing from the roster. Is there a mistake?" *After all, last season, I averaged ten points per game.* I genuinely thought he must have messed up somehow.

"Sorry, Ryan. You weren't good enough to make the top ten."

That was it. Cut.

Mad and embarrassed that some of my friends made the team when I didn't, I left the gym and headed home to tell my mom. I wanted to throw a pity party. But even back then, I knew negativity never fosters growth. Positive infinity was the way. Thirty-three years later, as the Head Coach of The Ohio State Buckeyes, the phrase "Positive Infinity" created by a few student-athletes became our mindset.

Mom gave me another gift at that moment when I was twelve years old. She never equated my worth as a human being with my performance. This consistent message grounded me. So, when I told her I didn't make the team, she took it in stride. She didn't get upset and call the coach. My parents taught me to address my coaches myself. They encouraged me to ask the appropriate questions to get the information I needed. Because of this perspective, when I said I didn't make the team, she calmly accepted the news, and we moved forward. Raising seven kids didn't give Mom and Pop Sal too much time to dwell on things. They had enough to handle. She left our things up to us to deal with.

Mom cared about *me*, not what I did or how many awards I won. All I ever knew from her was love. Same with my dad. They didn't care about the wins or losses. Of course, they knew how hard I worked and felt my pain when I lost. But I never once heard condemnation over the outcome of a competition. Mom believed in me, and Dad believed in me, which is a beautiful gift that instills confidence in a child.

Dad said, "There will always be some farm boy out there who works hard." I didn't believe him, but years later I found out he was right. His belief was life empowering. I didn't understand it then, but as a coach, I see the outcome of this belief and understand the life-changing nature of this gift. Doubt and negativity want to lodge themselves into our minds. We can't allow them to do so. I was ready to work harder to make that eighth-grade basketball team. I would start training immediately or maybe not.

1. What gifts did you receive from those who raised you?

2. What values in them or others did you admire?

3. What childhood memories can you reflect on that helped you foster a strong mindset?

4. Are there any childhood memories you need to let go of? How could you redefine these with Positive Infinity?

5. When did you experience your first disappointment over something that didn't turn out as you expected? What lesson(s) did you learn?

Chapter 2
Unanswered Prayers

Look beyond the moment, and you'll see the mountaintop

We have different gifts according to the grace given to each of us.

—Romans 12:6 NIV

How can something so heartbreaking become an opportunity for something even greater? The pain of not making the team disturbed my life. It disoriented me, but not enough to awaken me to something greater. It did, however, create another opportunity, one that would ultimately be foundational in my life.

While at dinner the night after I was cut from the basketball team, my older brother, Frank, told me I was going to wrestle. Up until then, basketball was my focus, and he knew that.

"Nope," I replied.

"Yes, you are," he shot back. What was he talking about? This was my closest friend. How could he suggest something so ridiculous?

"I love basketball, plus I've seen the uniforms, and I'm not going to wear that wrestling singlet."

"Aw, we only wear those in matches. Just come to practice tomorrow and give it a try. I think you'll be good at it," Frank said. He knew something I didn't. Maybe he thought all of the aggression I showed in the pick-up games on the school field might equate to something far better on a wrestling mat than a basketball court. Or perhaps it was the fact that I was never going to be more than 5'9" and at the time, I weighed seventy-five pounds and wasn't going to block too many shots against anyone.

I was a small kid. Because of my love for sports, I thought I'd play football. In the eighth grade, I practiced hard for one year but continued to get run over by bigger, faster people. My coach yelled at me to tackle the guy in front of me. At ninety pounds, I thought, *You tackle him! He's 175 pounds.* Football didn't make sense for me. I wanted to be great and knew early on that football wasn't going to work. The person who ended my football career was Scotty Graham. He was from a few towns over, and he ran over me time and time again. He ended up playing for Ohio State and then with the Minnesota Vikings. If you looked at him and then me, you'd agree that I used common sense by staying away from Scotty.

Frank was a great older brother and still is. There's so much value in being an older brother. I was blessed to have Frank. I was close with my younger sister, Kim, too. She wasn't a wrestler, although she did beat up one of my friends once. She was tough and still is.

Without knowing it at the time, my brother's push was the light of hope in what I thought was an unanswered prayer (not making basketball team). I went to wrestling practice, as he suggested.

That first wrestling practice made a ton of sense and changed the trajectory of my life. Coach Peppe and Coach Holle were the seventh-grade coaches, and their practice provided a foundation upon which I built my life. I was immediately hooked and got serious about the sport.

That seventh-grade year, I went 6-3 at the seventy-five-pound weight class. But the record wasn't as important as what I learned. This was a sport where any size person could flourish if they were willing to fight. We had so much fun traveling together on the school bus and laughing after matches, and we built lasting friendships. This taught me the team side of this individual sport. These connections made the sport more fun, and I loved it.

Brian Hooker was a teammate. His father took us to various tournaments and videotaped our matches. It was fun studying the films of what we did well and not so well. I'm grateful for Norm Hooker. He made a difference. Brian is now a coach at my old high school. He's giving back. I stay in touch with him and Jon Adwar, another former high school wrestling teammate. I'm grateful to many other high school wrestling teammates and the bonds that last a lifetime. Wrestling's struggles bonded us.

During the summer, I attended the J Robinson training camp at the University of Iowa, where I learned the value of suffering related to wrestling and life. These camps were a month-long, with four workouts every day. It was like being in boot camp. At least that's what Coach Robinson said. He was an Army Ranger as well as an Olympian.

Tom and Jay Robinson at the 2017 Big Ten Championships, The Ohio State's second Big Ten Championship in three years. One of my personal mentors in wrestling, J taught me to understand chosen suffering and its refining gifts.

Jay is one of the most influential men in wrestling's history. Not only was he a critical part of the Iowa dynasty, but he also eventually took over a weak program at Minnesota and turned it into a national powerhouse. Jay led with integrity and won three national titles there. His intensive camps touch many lives. A great example, he spent nearly the entire summer in a dorm room as campers of all ages learned suffering. Thousands of young men ran through this brutal training system.

Moreover, Jay and his three brothers fought in the Vietnam war together. Can you imagine the daily courage shown by the Robinson boys and the worry on their parents' hearts? American heroes. I cannot tell you the profound affect this man had on my life and so many others.

Jay transformed my mind and taught me and many others that we were capable of giving more than we ever thought. You are capable of so much more than you believe.

I learned the mental advantage you achieve when wearing out your opponent during a match. 6:30 a.m. runs were followed by 9:00 a.m. technique, live wrestling at 3:00 p.m., and finally an evening session mostly about how to operate under duress and fatigue. These camps tested our mind, body, and spirit. It was pure anguish. I needed it, and it elevated my understanding of what tough was.

The eighth-grade year was my second year of wrestling. Bernie Colombo, the varsity coach, saw me wrestle and asked if I wanted to move up to the varsity team to wrestle at the 103-pound weight class. I was so grateful for the opportunity. He was a great coach, and we're still close. He emails me after every one of my Ohio State team duals. We talk technique. I could have stayed on the eighth-grade team and wrestled kids my age, but that wouldn't help my progress enough.

I needed to be around better wrestlers who could expose my weaknesses. My brother was a sophomore and a leader on the team. I jumped at the opportunity and never looked back. Though I wasn't a high-level wrestler at this age, I understood effort mattered. I also liked there were weight classes, and my competitors were my size. Since I was small in a relatively large school, hanging around with seniors also provided some protection. Wrestling gave me a sense of belonging, identity, and purpose.

We all want to belong. If parents and coaches don't provide this belonging, this love, then some other group will. Love matters. Love sustains. People are drawn to love. It's the recipe for success on all great teams and great organizations.

Wrestling began to consume my life. It was my purpose for living. It was where I was most at peace. Six days a week, I either ran, lifted weights, or wrestled. On Sunday, mom took us all to St. Frances De Chantel church for mass. We were Catholic. I didn't like going, but Mom made us. I remember going to CCD classes too. A bunch of kids gathered once a week at someone's home and talked about God, Jesus, and His plan for our lives. I wasn't sure what to make of it all. I mean, I believed in something greater, but I never committed to that belief.

Deep trust takes a deeper inspection than my mind was ready to give. There were other decisions I needed to make that seemed more important at the time than who Jesus was. At that point, I was following orders. I went to learn because Mom said I had to. When we do something because someone else wants us to, it won't have a lasting impact on our growth until we make it ours. I only wanted to get back to wrestling and my friends. I didn't have time for God, at least not yet.

Wantagh High School Wrestling Team my ninth grade year. My brother, Frank, and I wrestled together on this team. Tom is front row left. Frank is second row left behind Tom.

My older brother and other teammates provided the fertile ground to chase my passion. I learned the value of hard work in a new, more intimate way. Being around the upper classmen committed to excellence pushed me. Kenny Meadows, a senior on my high school team, worked extremely hard. He was the best wrestler on the team, but more importantly, I noticed his work ethic. I always saw the hardest workers on every team I've ever been on. I always valued practice as sacred. I looked up to Ken. Working hard was always cool to me. I studied his training and asked him questions. He was five years older and told me of the J Robinson camps. I followed his lead. My brother, Frank, and I both did. Being a good follower matters. It matters more than you'd think.

Every summer, I went back to the J Robinson training camp at the University of Iowa. Being immersed in an environment that put me under duress and chosen suffering humbled me. It taught me the value of failing daily, giving more than I thought I could, and believing deeply in something greater than myself. I loved wrestling. I'd found my passion, what I call *my priceless*. Thank God for Mr. O'Leary, who shared truth with me by removing me from the seventh-grade basketball team.

An old Chinese proverb says, "If you want to fill the cup, you must first empty the old one." Too often we hold on to cups when they need to be emptied. Lifelong friends and true coaches willingly identify cups we need to empty. The Elite nurture these valuable relationships. They demand these relationships in their lives. They seek them out.

At this young age, I learned that conditioning is the universal equalizer in wrestling. You can't take an opponent to a place he isn't ready to go if you haven't taken yourself there first. It's simple, a tired man with great skill will struggle against an energetic, highly fit man with good skill. Repeatedly choosing to suffer is achievable through tempo and fitness. This understanding became a foundational pillar of my success to the point it wasn't even a conscious choice. Every step we take, we don't consciously thank gravity for its work in our life. It's just there. It always will be. Suffering became that for me.

Pain is relative. Suffering has varying levels and intensities. I knew about chosen suffering. That's the kind you bring upon yourself. It's the good and bad resulting from the decisions you make. You might call it the consequences of your actions— understandable and accepted. How we manage these types of pain is critical. We all choose the right and hard things but also wrong and easy things. The chosen suffering I refer to the most is the kind that moves us to a healthy place of discomfort. It's the choice to push your body past the point of fatigue—to a place it doesn't want to go—but you make it go anyway. This intersection is when growth begins to occur.

Chosen suffering can be brought on by poor choices as well. I've also learned the three necessary steps in correcting a poor choice. There's a healing process that needs to occur inside ourselves to help us move forward. The first step is to admit it. The second step is to apologize for it. The third and most challenging step is to let it go. Too many people hold on to poor decisions for too long. They carry guilt and regret, which grows heavy over time.

As humans, we comprehend chosen suffering. You control this suffering through effort. If you work hard, you believe you receive defined results reflective of your effort.

As I immersed myself in the wrestling world, this chosen suffering became my new normal. And once again, I saw the work-reward relationship. It was the challenge and love for this type of pain that was the greatest motivation.

Each year, I did better. Finally, in tenth grade, Frank and I won the Nassau County championship for our respective weight classes, which was a big deal. Few wrestlers in our area ever won this championship, so any county champion received incredible admiration. Getting to share this accomplishment with Frank was one of my treasured life moments. Truthfully, the admiration was far less valuable than the hard work that went into the sport.

We should be mindful of the weight we give to basking in the thoughtful comments of others, particularly those on social media. If you fall in love with the likes, then the hates will break you. Two-time Olympian and assistant coach Tervel Dlagnev, one of the great minds of the sport, shared this truth.

It's easy to get caught in this trap with social media. If this is the value system we take on, we must also be prepared for the hate from the same sources. This is a dangerous place for us to live. Sure, we all want people to like us, but our source of worth should always come from within.

As a sophomore, I finished fourth in the New York State championships. I was proud because I'd made huge strides and wrestled well. In my junior year, I lost a heartbreaking match in the semi-finals to finish third in the state finals. Funny how third can be depressing when the year before, fourth was so fulfilling. But I learned many lessons through that loss. After assessing and applying those lessons, I pursued my dream of being a state champion. All the pundits and statisticians predicted me to win in my senior year. On my part, I'd put in the hard work to be physically, mentally, and emotionally prepared.

However, unchosen suffering was moments away. In the first round of my senior state competition, I sustained a severe injury while leading 8-0. This injury smashed my dream in a single move—torn ligaments in my ankle. It was my first major setback. I was done, and my chance to compete for the state title was greatly reduced with only one leg. I'd done the preparation well, but hard work isn't always enough. My injury was out of my control. I didn't plan for it or cause it. Someone else intersected my life at that moment and changed my predicted trajectory. The first injury of my career came at the worst time. Years of hard work were seemingly lost. My dad took me to the emergency room the morning of the second day of the state tournament. We begged the doctors to numb it. They wouldn't as it was too dangerous for the long-term health of my leg. Forced to withdraw from the tournament, I was heartbroken.

Several college coaches dropped me as a recruit, which didn't make sense to me. Why would someone place their value in me solely on a competition where I couldn't walk? Why would they judge me at my weakest moment? Were they recruiting the person or the title? I was the same person with the same potential the day before the event as the day after the event.

The coaches who got to know me and my hunger for wrestling stuck with me. I'm grateful for them. We know love is the ultimate motivation, but at this moment, my desire to prove my potential and capability to all those who dropped me served as added motivation. Of course, this type of motivation will win in the short term, but, over time, our greatest motivation is the pure love of testing ourselves against the best. For a while, it would be anger and pain that fueled my improvement in the sport. To this day, not winning the state title bothers me.

When we experience a setback, we have two choices. We can wallow in the pain of the suffering and get stuck. Or we can also acknowledge what happened, deal with the pain, learn the necessary lessons from the experience, and move forward. Like all injuries, my ankle recovery took time to heal. However, recovering from the emotional pain of not meeting my goal took longer.

Returning from the state championships on crutches didn't help. It was difficult to answer questions about what happened and how I was doing. "I didn't win because I was injured" isn't an answer. I was mad and depressed. But my family was there for me, and I never felt condemnation or disappointment from those who loved me. Sure, they were bummed for me, but my value in their eyes wasn't based on winning. I never had to manage that type of stress. Winning doesn't make a man better than another. The true measure of a man should be based on how he treats others and how many he serves.

Wrestling had now been in my life for five years. I started in 1982, thanks to losing my spot on the basketball team. I graduated from Wantagh High School in 1987. I learned that it takes time to see the full picture of the plan for our life. It's easy to fall into the trap of narrow-sighted thinking. When you look beyond the moment, you'll see the mountaintop.

If one reads the page of my life that saw me fail in basketball tryouts, they might think I was a failure. Maybe they'd think I was a failure when I didn't win the state title. I've learned that we must step back and read the totality of our life's book to get a true understanding of unanswered prayers. For now, I would work harder to prepare for college wrestling.

1. Have you ever experienced a major setback? What was it and how did you go about dealing with it?

2. Do you have any unanswered prayers in your life and what are they?

3. What core qualities do you exhibit that will lead you toward attaining a goal? Which ones might hold you back?

4. Are there any cups in your life you should consider emptying? What would you fill them with instead?

5. What parameters have you placed on how you value others?

CHAPTER 3
CHANGING DIRECTION

Passion will bring you there; the priceless will keep you there

We all want progress, but if you're on the wrong road, progress means doing an about-turn and walking back to the right road; in that case, the man who turns back soonest is the most progressive.

—CS Lewis

The Elite understand how to cause discomfort—what I now call chosen suffering. It's always challenging because it's against our nature. Never willing to settle for the easy way, an Elite person constantly moves toward pain to push themselves beyond their current abilities. This healthy kind of chosen suffering bears the richest fruit when it is aligned with our purpose. Growth means stretching away from our comfort zone.

Chosen suffering is an outward display of what we love the most. We expend the most energy, time, resources, and focus on things we determine are most precious. Our energy and time are limited. Therefore, we should be conscious about what it is we value. Deep thought should go into our beliefs followed by actions that move us toward them.

Some people allow the barriers of living their dreams to be bigger than their desire to chase them. There are so many excuses that an improperly trained mind can make. Going into any big dream with the right attitude sets the stage for how long and intensely we'll continue to pursue it. Properly applied, chosen suffering fuels sustained success. It's the constant driver in life.

Over time, love's fuel will burn the cleanest and longest. Nothing stays the same—you either progress or regress. When you use this continuous pressure, you successfully move to the next plateau, whether in life, sports, business, or relationships. No one in our lives should demand a higher standard than the one we impose on ourselves.

Growth requires pain, which is why it's difficult to stay on top. It's too easy to reach the top and slip into complacency. But those who pursue true Elite-ness continue to reach just beyond their grasp. They pursue chosen suffering with laser focus.

I wanted to be on top of the wrestling world. After all my years of training during the summer at the University of Iowa, I hoped they'd call me. Unfortunately, I wasn't good enough to get noticed by Coach Dan Gable. He was and is a living coaching legend. He earned trust, which is the absolute necessity to progress.

The ankle injury at the New York tournament sealed my fate. Plus, a state title wouldn't have made a difference. A non-state champ wasn't going to get a call, nor was a state champ in a weight class they didn't need. The University of Iowa line-up carried multiple state champions, much like today's Ohio State University wrestling team.

However, past success and the achievement level don't always tell the entire story of a man's potential. As a coach, I've learned to look for the fire inside a man's heart. The Elite exhibit various traits, and success leaves clues. We need to seek them out and apply them consistently in our own lives.

I chose to attend and compete at Syracuse University alongside my brother, Frank, who was two years older. He was and still is one of my most impactful role-models. Frank was a team captain of the Syracuse wrestling team, law school grad, and recently, the chairman-elect of the law firm, DLA Piper. He's a first-generation college graduate. My brother never put a ceiling on himself. He didn't have many of the advantages that one might think to climb as high as he has. Excuses weren't part of his plan. Solutions were. He understands leadership, chosen suffering, and the timeless principles of success.

Those two years at Syracuse were great. I'm grateful my coaches, Ed Carlin and Gene Mills, believed in me despite my senior year injury. Frank and I wrestled together and shared a two-bedroom apartment. We competed back-to-back in the starting line-up—I was 150 pounds, and Frank was 158 pounds. I always felt more nervous for him than for my matches. Wrestling is a sport tailor-made for brothers.

I discovered a deep love for the sport and the bond forged not only with my brother but also with many other team-mates. Together we worked hard to make our mark among the wrestling Elite. As training partners, we fed off each other. Frank and I shared techniques and skills and grew together. We often spent Tuesday and Thursday nights taking the train into the city where we learned at the NYAC. We found the best place to learn and train alongside those who were equally passionate, though stronger and better skilled than us. This common pursuit brought us closer. To this day, despite our intense lives, we talk nearly every morning.

Even a simple, "Hello. All is good here," provides a reset button for us. This communication ensures our brotherly bucket will never run dry despite the myriad of other things that demand our time. I'm grateful Frank took his big brother role seriously. The world wants to beat us down—we need our homes and family to build us up.

Frank and his wife, Melissa, are amazing examples of this with their three sons, Zach, Sean, and Will. All three are athletes. Zach is a starter on Stanford men's soccer team for two years, which won the NCAA title when he was a freshman. Sean is on the Ohio State soccer team, and Will plays in high school. The power of example is real. Raising healthy and successful kids is far more likely when those who helped bring them into this life take responsibility for themselves and their children's lives.

In 1989, I won the EIWA (Eastern Intercollegiate Wrestling Association) Championship as a sophomore in the 150-pound weight class finishing the season with a 2-2 performance at the NCAA Division I Nationals. All my life, I've worked hard and looked for more in whatever I did. Wrestling was no different. The desire to be a Division I National Champion seemed just beyond my grasp. However, I continued to train, practice, study, and learn all I could to hone my skills. But something was missing. Questions haunted me. Could it have been my level of chosen suffering wasn't great enough? Was my goal of winning an NCAA title too lofty a goal?

The evening before our Syracuse team would compete at the Penn State Open in the winter of 1989, I decided to watch Iowa's team compete. They were competing against Penn State in a dual meet at the same venue we'd be in the next day. Throughout the entire two-hour competition, I was mesmerized by each wrestler's ability to focus. Each used a combination of speed and power to wear down their opponent. I knew this level of wrestling exceeded my own, and I wanted it.

This experience was my passion, something I refer to as *my priceless*. The ancients understood this concept in a different way and to a different level than most of us today. When asked to explain the meaning of my priceless, I often think back to the movie, *The Passion of the Christ*. If you're unfamiliar with the film, Jesus' passion was the cross—an ancient form of capital punishment. The cross—back then—was similar to our electric chair today.

It would be quite odd for us to describe a prisoner's passion for an electric chair. At first glance, it's also odd to think that Jesus' passion was the very instrument that would kill him. However, a deeper look reveals the mystery. The ancients defined passion as: how much you were willing to suffer for something. In other words: the level of passion is based upon the level of chosen suffering. Of course, Jesus' passion wasn't a wooden cross. Rather, it bridged the gap between the sin of the world and the love of his Father. His priceless wasn't the wood, it was the world.

For years, I dreamed of wrestling for Coach Dan Gable. The intensity these athletes competed with was something I longed for. At that moment, I knew I didn't have a choice. I had to leave Syracuse for Iowa to make this dream a reality. I hungered to be part of his program and life. He exuded excellence, and I wanted that.

This decision to switch direction changed my wrestling career and my life. Of course, I didn't know how my life would turn out except that I know following Elite principles over time leads us toward our best life. I realized I didn't want to be on my deathbed wondering if I reached my potential. I wanted to leave everything on the mat; a concept wrestlers say to explain, "giving your all."

It wasn't necessarily only about winning, but winning mattered. I needed to know I'd done everything to be the best wrestler I could be. While I believed in myself, I knew I could do more. Syracuse University was a tough program, with many hardworking men, but my gut instincts told me Coach Gable's well-documented system would take me to another level. I couldn't ignore the statistics. I needed a proven environment to help me submit to the deepest level of trust.

When I told my mom and my dad I was giving up my full-ride scholarship at Syracuse to walk-on at Iowa, they supported me once again. Dad told me he'd help me financially. Mom couldn't afford to, but she gave me something equally important—belief. She believed in me 100%, and that was something I could take with me to the "bank of life." I'd find out soon enough how much of a "withdrawal" wrestling for Iowa would require.

Syracuse was five hours from home. Iowa would be eighteen. My parents had to know they'd see me less, but they never allowed that to influence my decision. Love is so powerful. I wanted to be an NCAA Champion, and they backed me 100%. The hardest part about this decision was knowing I wouldn't wrestle with my brother any longer. Frank, who was entering his senior season at Syracuse, encouraged me to go. Headed for law school and always a better student, I jokingly said, "While Frank read books, I ran laps." My advice to all young people is to read.

Remember, pain is relative. The Elite understand attaining great things often means the more pain, the better. Sacrifice means we're giving something up for something else. It could be time, comfort, or a myriad of things. In my chosen suffering, I pushed myself to what I believed was the end of my limits. Gable's environment exalted this. Suffering has different aspects and levels. Chosen was familiar to me—the kind I caused—the good and bad. Each decision, right and wrong, brings pain. They're the product of our effort and the result of free will. Human beings understand this suffering. Wrestlers can make sense of it because the results depend on consistent effort. The greater and harder you work, the better the results usually are.

So, when school ended my Sophomore year, I packed my bags, let the Syracuse coaches know I was transferring to Iowa, the Mecca of college wrestling in the 80s and 90s, and threw my belongings in my car to drive from upstate New York to Iowa City. At the same time, there was a graduate from Iowa training in Syracuse. Royce Alger flew to Syracuse on an open-ended ticket to train with one of my Syracuse coaches, Chris Campbell. They pushed each other as they trained to make the Olympic team.

A brilliant technician, Chris taught me and others on the team so much. Chris made his second Olympic team in 1996 at the age of thirty-nine. Seventeen years earlier, in 1979, Chris was the world champ and favored to win the Olympic gold in 1980. When President Jimmy Carter boycotted the Olympics in 1980, Chris experienced the suffering that comes from working hard for your dream to have it snatched away. He understood heartbreak. He understood difficult. Eventually, I'd understand difficult and *tragic*. They're different.

When I let Royce know I was driving to Iowa, he decided to ride with me instead of flying back. "After all, two is better than one," I reasoned especially when it was a long drive in a car. Years later, I'd learn that three is an even sturdier bond than two. A cord of three is not easily broken.[2] Unchosen suffering would lead me to the bond of three. For now, I was focused on me. Time and circumstance would change that.

I didn't know Royce Alger personally, other than that he was bigger, stronger, and far more accomplished on the mat than I. As a world silver medalist and couple time National Champion, I admired him as an Elite wrestler. I looked up to him since I was a young man trying to make it in the sport. He'd accomplished what I was so hungry for. It was a long trip to Iowa City from Syracuse, NY. *The more drivers, the better. Plus, I'll get to hear some cool Dan Gable stories.* It seemed like a great plan.

We jumped into my red Ford Escort GT, and immediately, he did two things. First, he reclined the passenger seat and handed me a cassette tape to play. It was country music—his list of favorite songs. He loved George Jones, Hank Williams, George Strait, and others I wasn't familiar with. Growing up in New York, country music wasn't my style. In time, it became my favorite along with Christian rock, but until this time, I hadn't listened to these genres. I preferred classic rock and musicians like Michael Jackson, The Little River Band, The Cure, and maybe some Lou Rawls (Pop Sal loved his sound system in the house, and this was frequently on). But Royce insisted we listen to his country music. So, we did.

Leaving early evening, we didn't get to enjoy the beauty of upstate New York or the sunlight. Not long after we left Syracuse, Royce promptly fell asleep. Forget the good Dan Gable wrestling stories! I wouldn't hear them on this drive— just the continual snoring of a tough dude who'd been hit in the nose too many times.

I drove through the night. Because he slept, I figured it'd be safe to turn off the country music and tune into something to keep me awake and pass the time more quickly. My eyes felt heavy. There was no conversation, just good ole country music twanging about broken hearts and dreams. So, I turned on *my* music. As soon as I popped out that cassette tape and his music stopped, he woke up, opened his left eye, and told me to turn the music back on. Once I did, he fell back to sleep immediately.

We arrived in Iowa early in the morning after driving all night. He didn't drive a mile. When we got to his house, I slept for a few hours on his couch. I later checked into a motel, and the intense transformation was about to begin.

Royce had a savage mindset that I needed. He didn't put things on a pedestal. The NCAA tournament was a long and high reach for me, but Royce lowered it and made it more attainable in my mind. We have to win the mental battle before real progress can begin. Royce helped me navigate that process—others did as well. Like Olympic Champion, Randy Lewis, and Olympic silver medalist, Barry Davis.

Being around Elite people was such a blessing. It normalized things for me and helped me realize they were common men with an extraordinary desire. The lessons I learned gave me much-needed insight into what an Elite culture looked like and helped me build them at Hofstra and Ohio State. Under Gable, I witnessed a system of developing a culture applicable to any business.

Equally important was the physical preparation that'd fuel such a belief. I had finally arrived, and I was excited and ready. My *god*, the sport of wrestling was about to be elevated to a new level.

People matter. Choosing the right ones to be with matters. Pain unifies us, and love sustains us. I was now in the right place with the right people.

1. Do you need to change direction, and if so, what is holding you back?

2. What small steps can you put in place to begin to turn?

3. What are your current barriers that need to be knocked down for you to be your best version?

4. How would you describe your mindset toward the pursuit of your priceless?

5. When do you choose suffering, and when do you avoid it? Why?

6. What people in your life should you move toward to get better? Up until now, why have you chosen not to?

CHAPTER 4
PAIN PRECEDES PROMOTION

The #1 indicator of sustained success is emotional control

Courage is not having the strength to go on; it is going on when you don't have the strength.

—Theodore Roosevelt

I headed west from New York to Iowa, and there was no looking back to the east. I knew this was going to be extremely difficult, and I was mentally prepared for what was ahead. I was ready to train alongside some men who exemplified the highest standard of excellence.

Having been to summer camp at the University of Iowa, I knew my way around town and headed to the wrestling practice room. Summers in Iowa were hot!

Little did I know the next few hours would be pivotal. I'd discover whether or not I had the inner fortitude to become Elite. Was becoming Elite something I was willing to truly pay for? So many of us want something but apply our set of rules rather than the proven rules. We program our minds to believe something is a certain way then apply only the facts that fit this thinking. When intense resistance arrives, disaster and excuses follow.

Simply put, we rationalize and then settle for less. Denial is a coping mechanism that ultimately sabotages sustainable success. It's a brain inhibitor that stops us from being solution-focused. We have to combat this. We must be willing to adapt to the real truth of what's necessary—not our truth. Fighting our way through the real truth is the part of the journey that results in growth.

An Elite minded person applies timeless principles. I call them Traits of the Elite. As a coach, my belief in a student-athlete grows when I observe these traits and principles displayed consistently. Therefore, one-offs mean little. Elite people understand that short bursts of choosing the right way don't make enough of a difference. Sometimes things can seem overwhelming, so we start the transformation with something simple. Building habits take time. The answer to the question of how do you eat an elephant? It's accurate to say, "One bite at a time."

Deep-rooted good habits must be formed. It's the long-term, sustained commitment that turns normal into special. Show up and give over and over. I tell my team to develop a two-word sentence that calms the mind from unraveling during tough things. It's a mantra. Mine was, keep working. Keep working.

In June 1989, I had just turned twenty years old. Gable's teams were fierce, and they wrestled in a style and manner I often dreamed about. To compete as they did, I knew I had to immerse myself in their world of discomfort. I came to learn there's no such thing as outrunning discomfort. It'll always come. Discomfort shows its face during intense training, intense studying, rehabbing an injury, building one's business, raising a family, managing people, and so on. Not every moment will be like this, but certain times bring struggle.

It's the men or women willing to not only bring themselves to this place but also remain stoic and execute during the battle that has the best chance to prevail. In essence, it's the ability to stay calm in the storm. The more storms we face and seek, the better we can deal with the challenges these storms bring. I know, it sounds better talking about it than actually going through them. But the most beneficial learning occurs when we're personally afflicted.

Standing on the outside looking in offers one important perspective, but it's less beneficial than the view when immersed in it. There was no internet back in 1989 to share secrets. The only way was to feel it, live it, and move into Dan Gable's training world. It was a simple decision, really. At least for me during that season of my life. Gable's way would be my way.

In any field, business, or sport, the Elite choose to be mentored by the best whenever possible. History doesn't lie. Extraordinary rarely develops in a bubble. The Elite surround themselves with others who help them master their craft. Deep love for one's craft needs to be watered by others who are like-minded. But it often takes a deeper love to empower us to do what most won't.

Today I refer to this decision as chosen suffering. If you want to know how much success you'll have in any endeavor, ask yourself how much you're willing to suffer to achieve it. If you're not willing to pay a high price but are looking for a quick solution instead, you're headed down a road to nowhere. Chosen suffering is synonymous with love and sacrifice. The best in any area willingly pay a price that others won't. They're masters in the details. It's not magic. It's actually simple. They'll give what others weren't willing to during practice and elsewhere. Details matter. We often *get* in direct proportion to what we *give*. This applies to all of life and every relationship.

The Elite are curious. They're thinkers and problem solvers with a growth mindset. They're never stuck, and they improve, plan, act, assess, and repeat. They're intelligent and show initiative. They're curious and move toward the right people rather than away. They're tough-minded seekers. They understand the power in the perfect alignment between being optimistic and realistic. They walk that tight rope between the two.

My first workout after driving from Syracuse to Iowa was a soul-cleanser. I collapsed in my car outside the Carver-Hawkeye arena after completing my first training session inside the Iowa wrestling room. I couldn't stop crying. I'm not sure whether it was the embarrassment, exhaustion, the thought of how far away I was from my goal, or feeling sorry for myself. Whatever it was, it was painful. Humiliating.

My body's core temperature was higher than the interior of my red Ford Escort GT. The Iowa summer sun baked my car as I sat inside it on the vinyl seats, trying to process what just occurred. There were traces of my blood sprinkled across my sweat-drenched grey shirt. The long drive through the night didn't bring me what I expected. My arms were so tired I could barely lift them to wipe my eyes and start my car.

My neck muscles were so exhausted that my head felt like a 100-pound bowling ball being supported by a narrow toothpick. I could barely look up with my eyes. Every muscle in my neck was utilized to total muscular failure. This level of intensity far exceeded my preparation to this point. I didn't think this scenario was possible. I was broken. I thought I was closer to being Elite, but I was wrong. But I loved the truth— acceptance of truth is powerful and essential for progress.

My pride took the worst beating. Since I always envisioned myself as the fittest wrestler, that practice was a dismal failure. The second floor of Carver Hawkeye Arena was a brutal place. The new Jennings Center on the campus of Ohio State University is a brutal place, too. It has to be. We focus on developing talent. The people in the facility must generate greater opposition than anything one can face outside the room.

Conversely, our homes must also create love so strong that nothing outside can make us feel less than we're worthy of. The men in that Iowa room in 1989 were tough. We had eleven All-Americans for ten weight classes. The coach was tough, too—and tender. He was special. Dan Gable never wasted a word during my time there. This small group of Elite men had beaten me with a dose of reality on this first practice day. I learned how I stacked up against the best, which was the truth I needed.

Seeking raw truth is powerful. Later in life, I'd pursue this search for truth more vigorously than my ability to become an Elite wrestler. I've always been simple, only wanting the truth. That mindset continually searches for facts and associates with others who can provide them. During this ninety-minute practice, I learned plenty of truths. Dan Gable's practice room was my new wrestling "factville."

Tom, University of Iowa Wrestling Team, 1992

Faced with these new truths during the past ninety-minutes, my mind nearly unraveled. I stood at a crossroad. My first practice started well but took a terrible turn. At 2:30 p.m., after my all-night drive, I entered the University of Iowa wrestling room to show myself and Dan Gable how I would help the Hawkeyes win more Big Ten and NCAA Titles. What started with high expectations and confidence, ended in my current position—crying in my car. All alone. Just me and my rear-view mirror.

I've witnessed this same scenario as a coach. It's a beautiful thing to see passion and resilience in a man. Some won't take themselves to the deep, ugly place. However, when they do and keep coming back for it, I know they're going to get results.

Myles Martin, a freshman NCAA champion for Ohio State, experienced this the summer before his freshman year. My staff brings our recruits onto campus in early June to prepare them for the late August start of the season. We want to learn about them and their willingness to give. Myles came in as the nation's top recruit. His first training session at Ohio State found him hunched over the garbage pail.

He went to a level of discomfort that extended his norm. I was excited for him. He had so much success, and despite it, he was going to climb levels if he only kept coming back. And he did. That following March, he became one of the few men to ever win an NCAA title right out of high school. He endured, showed up, worked hard, accepted truth, and applied it. It's not hard to spot motivation. It stands out even in the grittiest places.

True freshman Myles Martin celebrates after defeating Bo Nickal in the 2016 NCAA Finals held at Madison Square Garden. He was the 15ᵗʰ true freshman in NCAA history and the first ever at The Ohio State to win the NCAA championship title. His freshman year journey was filled with chosen suffering.

Though I didn't know a single person on the Iowa team, I *knew about* a few of them. Keep in mind, there was no internet to share information about various student athletes or to highlight those brilliant gladiators in the sport. If you didn't know someone with a VHS tape featuring an Elite wrestler, you couldn't watch wrestling, except for the rare occasion it was broadcast on the Wide World of Sports, which is how I watched several of these men in the 1984 Olympic Games.

The Brands brothers were big names at Iowa who earned respect due to their ferocious style, which I wanted to emulate. Each eventually won several NCAA titles, World Titles, and Olympic gold and bronze. We still compete against each other as they're the head and assistant head coach at the University of Iowa. I know them well. They were tough and still are. To defeat a mindset like theirs, it helps to understand it. Living alongside them gave me valuable insight. We were all seniors together in 1992 and won two NCAA team titles in 1991 and 1992.

As I sat in the corner of the room—the one I knew so well from summer camps—it began to fill with bodies, and my nervous energy increased. Anytime we're going to put ourselves under intense discomfort, there's a nervous energy that happens. It's kind of scary in a good way. Progress has an element of pain to it. The room was black and gold, with names of wrestling legends on all the walls. The giant Hawkeye head stared at me. I loved it.

Coach Dan Gable walked over to where I was sitting and asked who I was. I told him my name, that I would be enrolling in school in the Fall, and would like to walk-on (no athletic scholarship) to his team. I was free for the program, but free is only useful if it has substance and can hold over time. Wrestling as a 150-pounder, Coach Gable didn't need me because sophomore Doug Streicher had placed fifth in the nation. A homegrown Iowa boy, he'd just earned All-American honors placing fifth in the nation that March. He was a great mat wrestler, with a challenging style of wrestling. I respected him as a team member but also as a tough opponent who I was likely to battle for the starting spot. We both had two years of eligibility remaining.

Coach Gable's next words were, "Okay. Well, you're not going to get any better sitting there. Why don't you jump in with the Steiner brothers over there."

I didn't know who they were, but I glanced where he pointed. Coach knew who they were and chose to test me against a few *animals*. These two were God-loving men who lived disciplined lives and loved wrestling. They were fitness freaks raised in North Dakota. My dad warned me about the guys who lived in the middle of nowhere, and all they did was wrestle. I thought he was joking, but I found out he wasn't.

They were the standard by which toughness could be measured. Just like the Brands, they were identical twins. They were one year younger and smaller than me. This should have been an advantage for me as the heavier man. As true freshmen who completed their redshirt seasons (a year the NCAA allows a student-athlete to train but not compete for the varsity team), Troy Steiner was a 134 pounder, and Terry Steiner a 142 pounder. At 150 pounds, I should have had an advantage.

Both of these brothers made differences in many people's lives. Troy Steiner is now the head coach at Fresno State University. Terry is the Head Olympic Coach of Team USA Women's program. Dan Gable's coaching tree is immense and embedded in the culture of American wrestling. Troy and Terry have remained friends of mine. They're amazing men, critical in my development. They never felt sorry for me. They were unemotional about their effort toward anyone who stood across the mat from them. They gave what they could every time. As a training partner, one either raised their level of toughness or took the brunt of theirs. It was a choice. We all get to pick one. I chose to fight.

Coach Gable started the workout with a drill, which meant we practiced our moves on each other. A common practice in all wrestling rooms is to work together with little resistance against one another. This repetitive practice helps muscle memory, builds the cardiovascular system, and the athlete's reactions. Coaches use this type of drilling to warm up the muscles and get the team ready for live wrestling.

There was something different about this drill though— the pace. The tempo was furious. Generally, during a drill, an attack occurs approximately every eight to ten seconds. With the Steiner brothers, an attack occurred every three to five seconds. This drill continued for roughly forty-five minutes.

My body and mind grew tired. I hit a threshold of exhaustion, resulting in my inability to control any deliberate movements. My mind unraveled as Gable and his staff looked on. Fortunately, Coach yelled the most coveted word on the planet when extreme fatigue hits, "Time."

I was exhausted and relieved. I realized I'd barely made it through this intense and exhausting drill. Winners don't just make it through. They thrive. The Elite thrive in the toughest environments. The Steiner's were thriving. I wasn't. They didn't seem tired at all, but I was dying. My heart rate spiked to a level that caused the lack of oxygen to my brain and muscles. The Elite never want to be in scenarios where the stakes are high and their preparation is below the level of challenge. We'll always sink to the level of our training. It's a Navy Seal creed, but it's also truth. Unfortunately, I lived that scenario during that training session.

I honestly thought practice was over after coach yelled, "Time." I was wrong. The next thing Gable said sent chills down my spine.

"You should all be warm by now and ready to start practice?"

Warm?

Start?

I was well beyond warm. I was finished. My legs wobbled, and my upper body lacked the strength I had when I entered the building so sure of myself. It's interesting how tough we can feel before and after practice. I want the man who's tough during it, which wasn't me on this day. When the moment we're so excited about comes, we have to remind ourselves, *This is what you said you wanted.*

> WHERE WE FIND DIFFICULTY WE MAY ALWAYS EXPECT THAT A DISCOVERY AWAITS US.
> CS LEWIS

My mind played tricks on me that day. Deep suffering is far more fun to talk about than live. Unless, of course, you want to be Elite. Then, there's no other option. I was learning how one person's suffering was laughable for another. It was all about perspective.

How many times had each person demanded that they respond to something difficult? The more times, the better. I knew I could use what I was born with to harvest something greater. Greatness is developed. That's why I came to Gable and his program. It's the same reason why my current Ohio State team is filled with hungry men. They know we'll develop them and transform them if they *choose* to suffer. Those who decide not to choose this will never get there, but those who choose to suffer have a chance.

Gable planned to have us wrestle in groups of three for the next part. But this was full thrust work, and practice drills were long gone. This was a straight-up fight with rules. Number one wrestled two, and then two wrestled three. The Steiner's and I continued to wrestle together. However, what started okay didn't last long. Within five minutes, they were beating me unmercifully, and I was exhausted. They didn't care that I was a new guy. Clearly, they weren't on the welcoming committee.

There was no coffee mug and a thank you note, and they didn't care about picking on someone bigger than they were. Their focus was to prepare for the toughest scenario an opponent could throw at them. They focused on hardening themselves. If I was the nail, they were the hammer. For roughly sixty minutes, they scored on me at will. If they weren't identical twins, I would've thought I was seeing double. By the end, I was utterly broken.

As I sat crying in my car, I thought about what Coach Gable must have been thinking. In the exhaustion, my mind played tricks on me. When we experience disappointment, our thoughts spiral, and it's important in those moments to press pause and assess the situation, not be led by our emotions. *The #1 indicator of sustained success is emotional control.* We must keep the issue in the appropriate bucket. Too often, we allow issues from one part of our lives to overflow into another. Therefore, pressing pause at such a time is crucial.

Thankfully, at that moment, I pushed pause to consider my options. I could drive back to Syracuse. My coaches there would gladly allow me to return. I was the reigning EIWA Champ with a redshirt and two more years of eligibility. However, when my tears and emotions got under control, I thought more clearly. When you're under emotional duress, it's not a good time to make any decisions. I've seen lives ruined over emotional decisions.

I drove back to the motel in the heat of my car, processing what happened. I assessed, made a plan, and took action. Humans will get nowhere unless they compile information, make a plan, and act on it. Not doing so is a formula for madness.

I had data from the workout. The Steiner's were stronger and more fit than I. Therefore, they tired me out and took advantage of that fatigue. It's a simple, timeless truth: A tired man is at a massive disadvantage over a man who isn't. They weren't only stronger, but their skills were better than mine on the mat. They were incredibly hard to escape from. The Steiner brothers exposed more holes than anyone did in my first two years at Syracuse University. So, I knew I was in the right place in Iowa.

Isn't this what we desire?

Don't we need to see our blind spots so we can overcome them? In the days, weeks, and months to come, truths confronted me. If I cared enough, those truths would become my teachers. If I willingly chose to suffer, I'd transform into a better me. I craved that.

Pulling into the motel parking lot, I made up my mind. If I planned to become an Elite wrestler, this was the place to do it. I promised myself I've never be this tired again. Instead, I chose to suffer more often and even deeper.

That day, the Steiner's and others along my journey showed me love. Feeling sorry for someone doesn't necessarily help them. Chosen suffering is rooted in unwavering passion and love. After a good meal and a long nap, I returned to the wrestling room to lift and run.

The real journey was about to begin.

> GOOD LEADERS CULTIVATE HONEST SPEECH; THEY LOVE ADVISORS WHO TELL THEM THE TRUTH.
> PROVERBS 16:13
> THE MESSAGE

My mind moved from one place to another. I wasn't giving myself a way out. I knew this was going to take time and tremendous effort. Good to great isn't an overnight thing. The only way to transform is to earn it.

I was staying, and chosen suffering would be my guide.

1. As you look at your life, where are you complacent?

2. How do you define chosen suffering?

3. Can you remember a crossroad in your life? How did you manage? What did you learn from it?

4. Have you ever been angry at someone for trying harder than you? Why?

CHAPTER 5
THE CHASM FROM BELIEF
TO COMMITMENT

Elite people have a
bias toward action

Happy is a man who finds wisdom and who acquires
understanding, for she is more profitable than silver, and her
revenue is better than gold. She is more precious than jewels;
nothing you desire compares with her.

—Proverbs 3:13-15 CSB

Six months later, in December of 1989, I focused on becoming the best wrestler in the country in my weight class. I completely committed to it. It was almost life or death for me. At least that was how it felt at the time. Transitioning from a believing mind to committed actions is a massive chasm most of us need to sort out. We must figure out what the barrier is between believing and committing.

The empty Greyhound bus had a few occupying the fifty available seats. The ride home from Iowa City, Iowa, to Long Island, New York, took forever. It was 1,031 miles and a straight shot east along I80. However, Greyhound buses stop in various cities along the way. We occasionally veered slightly north or south of I80 to pick up or drop off passengers.

Since we didn't have cell phones or the internet, bus riders spent the time reading, reflecting, or listening to music on a CD player or the radio. I did a bit of each, tired from my grueling first semester since transferring to the University of Iowa.

The men in the Iowa wrestling room extended my ability to endure discomfort and helped move me forward. Though enormous, the intensity and work load was worth it. My full trust in the system produced progress. Trust always precedes real progress.

The University of Iowa had won fifteen NCAA titles under Dan Gable and twenty-one consecutive Big Ten titles along with a long list of individual NCAA champs and Olympic champs. Inspecting Gable's ability to produce winners revealed plenty of logical facts that led me to trust him and his system.

Classes were over for a few weeks during Christmas break and training would resume again on December 26. This trip home would only be for a few days, as I was competing in a tournament on December 29.

This short time was about family, gift giving, and laughter. Our big family loved to get together and celebrate with great food, great conversation, poker, board games, and great friends from the neighborhood. Santa Claus always showed up too. Since I'd been away from home for six months, I couldn't wait to see everyone.

Having made the transition from Syracuse University to Iowa, I fought for relevancy on a team that history would show was one of the best ever. The first semester was as hard as I expected it would be. Showing improvement by closing the gap on the Elite wrestlers around my weight class, I felt settled into the team.

I learned that big talk won't earn respect. The way to earn respect was to compete. Consistent actions build respect, not words. I worked to develop my mass—that sense of who you are—into something that pulled others in. Since I was attracted to those who were tough and real, my roommates were Terry Brands, one of the more ferocious competitors in NCAA history, and Travis Fisher, a hard-nosed, small town Iowa boy. They asked me to room with them, and I jumped at the opportunity. I based every decision on principles that would lead me to greatness on the mat. Terry and Travis were blessings to live with as both had jumped the gap from believing to committing. I've learned Elite people have a bias toward action.

From my earliest memories, I moved toward those types of people. The Iowa wrestling room was no different. There were levels of sacrifice displayed every day among this team of forty men. Some believed and some were committed. There's a big difference. The large gap that separates the two is called action. Committed means your life reflects your beliefs and I was committed.

I spent my mornings, afternoons, and most evenings in the wrestling room. I trusted and acted on the trust. I moved toward the top ten percent of the Elite, and they moved toward me.

Sitting on that Greyhound bus looking out the window, I watched the trees pass and followed the road beneath the bus tires. Leaving my older brother and teammates along with a full scholarship at Syracuse was tough, but I knew I'd made the right decision. Iowa offered no scholarship, only an opportunity. I was determined to make sure my work reciprocated the love and support I'd been given from my family.

I believe the measure of a man's work will reflect in the way he competes. Effort is the master informant to all who watch. It offers clarity to the viewer. The rate at which a person works is a window into the soul of what he values as priceless in his life. Both the professional eye and the novice sees the clear connection between effort and the workload that occurs when few are watching.

I didn't get home often once I left for Iowa. The thousand-mile journey offered me plenty of time to reflect. I came home less than five times during my three years for a total of three weeks. My life became extremely focused on what I needed, which was mostly in Iowa City. I made some strong friendships, and life was as much fun as it was intense.

Perhaps the biggest and most helpful decision I made was to move up a weight class. I started the 1989 season at 150 pounds and succeeded there. I won over the 1988 NCAA finalist and managed a few wins over the current starters on the team. I wasn't sure, but I thought that Coach Gable began to see me as a potential starter for the next season. Of course, with this level of talent and desire in the room, any level of latency would cause someone to get passed by. I was catching up, but I couldn't rest on the success of yesterday.

In late December, the increased muscle I added moved me into the 158-pound weight class. I felt great at that weight and focused on lifting more than running. I loved to lift weights, so this was a great change.

The long bus ride allowed plenty of time to think about the things in my life that mattered. My family and wrestling were at the top of the list. While reflecting on the end of the first semester and my excitement about my progress and new weight class, we pulled into a bus terminal in Chicago, Illinois.

I was red-shirting that season, which means you practice with the team but can't compete in Varsity events. I'd wrestled two seasons as a starter at Syracuse University, and due to NCAA transfer rules, I was forced to sit out. I had a redshirt year plus two years of eligibility remaining.

I was seated toward the back-left side of the relatively empty bus when the doors opened. There were only a few of us, and we all stayed on. As the new faces boarded, one was a Catholic priest. His attire showed me who he was committed to. Hoping he'd choose another row to sit in, I did my best not to make eye contact with him. I was far enough to the back of the bus that it seemed logical that he'd choose a seat with an entire row available. I was wrong. He sat directly next to me and stayed there most of the way from Chicago to New York. Because I wanted the extra space, I remember not being overly happy.

The conversation was actually quite engaging. The Catholic priest shared the things he believed and loved, and his deep commitment to his faith. He shared his passions with me. In turn, I shared mine with him. He shared the gospel with me and the love God has for me. I engaged in the conversation but couldn't quite get my mind to commit to a faith like his because he shared his conclusions not mine. He had searched. I had not. I was not surprised by how much he knew and how much thought he poured into this before he trusted. I believed him, but not enough to inspect whether or not God is real. It didn't matter much to me. I guess I felt like I didn't need to search.

There's a massive chasm between believing something and committing to it. Believing a chair will hold us is one thing. But until we actually sit in the chair, it's only a belief. At that moment, I wasn't ready to sit in the chair and commit to God. I chose to commit to the "chair" that would build my wrestling career.

Of course, these two searches could have co-existed. However, I wasn't in enough pain to quiet the world. My suffering was chosen by me and all about me. I focused on what was most pressing in my life at this time—developing as a wrestler.

If we want real progress and submission to occur, we must cross this massive bridge from believing something to committing to that belief. To conquer something large, we simply take one step at a time. The first step involves surrendering to the truth that our current way may not be the best way. But I was too busy with other decisions to do the intensive search to move from believing in God to committing to Him.

As we pulled into the Penn Station terminal in New York City, we said goodbye and went our separate ways. He shared his knowledge, his love, and his assuredness that Jesus had a place for me in His home if I'd accept it. It was a home for all those who accepted His love. I listened and believed then moved my mind back into the world where I lived.

Chosen suffering was the world that ruled my thoughts: my choices, my life, and my control of what's next. The trust in the priest's voice intrigued me. He was so sure about what he told me because he spent his life researching it. He was completely committed to it, and I was confident about what I was telling him too. Each of us believed and committed to the message we conveyed and our purpose. We both made progress on our chosen paths because of that commitment. I knew how to train and become Elite at wrestling. Gable was teaching me that. We both held onto the truths we explored. As I walked in the front door of my home, I quickly put aside the conversation on the bus. It was great to be home, even temporarily.

Within a week after I returned to Iowa City from New York, I defeated Pat Smith at the Midwest Classic. I wasn't aware of how good Pat was.

After my late December win over Pat Smith, Gable called me into his office to tell he'd give me some scholarship money. I was so thrilled, not about the money, but about being called into his office. It meant he noticed my progress. He gave me three hundred dollars for the second semester, which was enough to pay for my books the second semester. The following season, he offered me a full-tuition scholarship. As soon as I got back to my dorm room, I called my dad and brother Frank to share the good news. It was a great moment.

Chosen suffering, deeply rooted in my love for the sport and deep trust in Coach Gable, was working. Committing to a well-constructed belief gave me a chance to attain my dream.

1. Make a list of what you believe.

2. Make a list of the things you've committed to and the things you want to commit to but haven't. Why haven't you committed yet?

3. What process do you use to determine whether or not something is believable?

4. Have you ever been convinced that something was a truth and found out later that your assessment was wrong? What were the circumstances?

5. Have you ever found out something was believable that you didn't think much about before? What was it and why?

6. What causes you to consider the things that you pour your thoughts into?

Chapter 6
Mind Drift

An attacking mindset always prevails

There can be no deep disappointment where there is not deep love.

—Martin Luther King, Jr.

D eciding to choose to suffer becomes the norm in the life of anyone choosing to be Elite. The power of suffering is well-documented throughout history on its cleansing effect on our life. At some point for an Elite performer, it moves from the conscious to the subconscious. It becomes part of the process. This type of suffering involves intentional, consistent, and well-defined outcomes. I set the goal, determined the steps necessary to achieve that goal, and worked hard to eliminate anything that deters from achieving that goal.

When I decided to leave Syracuse, I committed myself to whatever suffering was necessary to achieve the goal. *Trying* to make it wasn't in my thought process. In that decision, I reinforced my priceless—to become an Elite wrestler under Coach Dan Gable's tutelage. Surprisingly, that decision wasn't difficult. I pursued my goal under the coach who had the most success.

High school and my injury left me hungry for college.

When I first arrived in the Iowa wrestling room in June 1989, I got beat up badly almost every day. It didn't matter what size teammate I wrestled. My body couldn't hold up to the amount of energy they threw at me. My teammates were better prepared. I didn't like it, but I learned, and I was grateful for the lesson.

We started every workout in the bleachers with a quick talk from Coach Gable. Afternoon practice was roughly two hours on the mats, along with a run or skill workout in the morning. Usually, I returned to the room in the evening to get a lift in, sit in the sauna to recover from the day's work, and prepare my body for what was next. They were long days, but they had to be. If I wanted to make the starting team and a difference in the program, there was no other option. With all the talent on the team and only ten weight classes for forty men, most of the team desired Elite-ness. If I wanted a spot on the team, I had to step it up.

Small gains came, and I held onto each one. I formed small, non-negotiable habits previously not part of my life. Deeply in love with wrestling now, I assessed every aspect of the sport to identify where I could make gains. Making sure I chose my weekly training partners every Monday would ensure I had the right partner to challenge me. I wanted to be deeply challenged in every practice. Sunday, I made my meals for the week—grilled chicken and pasta were cheap, simple, and nutritious. I don't remember ever eating fast food. When I had a day full of classes, I filled my backpack with veggies to make sure I had the energy I needed to thrive in practice.

In 1991, we had nine All-Americans and six in the NCAA finals. In 1992, we also had nine All-Americans and a host of NCAA champs. Despite winning the Big Ten in 1991 and 1992, I didn't win the NCAAs. The best I could do was second and third.

In my junior year, I was far better prepared than my senior year. I faced Pat Smith in the finals, the man who I had previously beaten. This time, I lost 7-6. Pat became the first four-time NCAA champion. I was winning with less than thirty seconds to go when we went out of bounds. To this day, I remember every thought and every second of every position.

A few nights before the NCAA finals, I had dinner with my technical coach, Jimmy Zalesky. Jimmy was a three-time NCAA champ who helped me, as did his older brother, Lenny. These brothers were tough and technical. They're great men who are both college head coaches and good friends.

When I went out of bounds, I remembered the conversation between Jimmy and me the week before. I asked him what it felt like to win his first title. As my opponent and I walked back to the center, I allowed my brain to recall that previous evening's conversation. As soon as my foot was on the line in the center of the mat, the referee blew the whistle. Pat shot and got to my ankle. A scramble ensued, and he came out on top with twelve seconds to go. I fought hard to get out, which sent the match into a tough back and forth battle in the final seconds.

Ultimately, I couldn't escape and lost the NCAA final match. That was the biggest loss of my life. I squared up with my foot on the line, thinking I was seconds away from winning. I had the mindset of protect and defend. Simultaneously, Pat squared up, thinking he was seconds away from also winning. He had the mindset of attack and score. It was a battle of mindsets, and his prevailed.

Of course this is true. Today when we recruit a wrestler, we assess many attributes. One critical trait is their attack rate.

The offensive wrestler who takes a well-practiced shot will statistically outperform the wrestler who protects and defends.

I remember Gable putting his arm around me as I walked off the stage of the NCAA final. I wanted that win so badly. I was so close. How could I have allowed my mind to drift during the biggest moment and event of my life?

I didn't come to Iowa for Big Ten titles. I didn't even consider them. I came for NCAA Titles and fell short.

There was an emptiness in me.

Though I wasn't lost, I was hurting. What I came to Iowa for alluded me. A last-second loss as a junior and an injury-riddled senior year left me in an empty place. So much went into winning.

What would college leave me hungry for? It would leave me so close but never attaining what I deeply longed for.

After the NCAA's my senior year, I worked in the Amana colonies on an assembly line where I shaved down parts for refrigerators. Working eight hours on the night shift felt like I was punishing myself for not winning. I was angry and empty for a while, numbing myself with work that was simple and repetitive. Every thirty-seconds I received a part on my spot on the assembly line. I grabbed it, shaved down any sharp edges, and placed it back on the line.

My identity was so wrapped up in who I was as a wrestler and my vision quest to become an NCAA champ. I calculated most of my life around practice times and being prepared physically and mentally for them. I planned when and what I ate and every partner I'd train with and why. I learned to control all the things I could. The margin of error between good and great and attaining the goal or missing it was so narrow.

Some time passed after my senior season when Duane Goldman, a former Iowa legend, asked if I'd be interested in coaching with him at Indiana University. Though I wasn't sure if I was called to coaching or not, I drove the six and a half hours from Iowa City to Bloomington for an interview.

I really liked Duane, his desire to build a winning program, and decided to pursue college coaching.

I liked Bloomington, Indiana. We had some good guys on the team who were committed to excellence. Looking back, I wasn't ready for coaching as I was immature and unable to lead anyone. I could wrestle hard, and I understood many important aspects of the sport, but I wasn't too sure about who I was and what I wanted. As a team, we fought for respect. I fought to shrink the empty feeling I carried. I needed to make sense of my life. I stayed for two years, just long enough to create an opportunity that would bless me a year later. Indiana gave me the coaching experience I desperately needed.

During the second year at Bloomington, I met my wife, Lynette, and her one-year-old son, Jordan. They changed my life in many ways. She was beautiful and honest. I wasn't ready for this in my life as my *core* wasn't quite strong enough. Jordan, who I eventually adopted, was amazing. He was so smart and made life better.

We would hang out together often. I loved to be with him. As a young child, I saw a brilliance in him, a unique mind. As his life unfolded, he proved that belief. A relentless reader, he seemed to have total recall. Jordan's 36 ACT score on reading and writing didn't surprise us. He graduated from the Fisher School of business and is on the executive team of a wrestling apparel company called RUDIS. This company of humble beginnings, founded by Jeff Jordan, Jesse Leng, and Tommy Rowlands, is now an international brand. We are very proud of the transformations in Jordan's life and his ability to lead his team.

Eventually, when I decided to leave coaching and compete again, we got married and moved to the small town of Hills, Iowa, which is south of Iowa City. Before we knew it, Lyn was pregnant with Jake, and our family was growing. I was growing too, now responsible for three lives beside my own.

I was waiting on tables a couple of days a week and earning a small stipend from the Hawkeye wrestling club. We had a small house out in the country, and we were happy, but finances were tight. Like most couples starting out, we had to work together and stay together. As a waiter, I wasn't bringing in a lot of money, and the Hawkeye club couldn't pay much other than assist with training expenses. We started our family, had no health insurance, and struggled to make ends meet. Things weren't working so well. I remember my conversation with Coach Gable. His honesty gave me some great clarity.

Wanting big things for our lives simply isn't enough. We need a deep obsession to act on what we desire. It's chosen suffering and self-learning through the deepest desire to prevail. Toward the end of my first-year wrestling for the Hawkeye wrestling club, a job at Hofstra opened up. The Athletic Director called me for a meeting about their program. A few Hofstra alumni called as well. A good friend, Guy Truicko, wanted to help me get the position.

Coach Gable knew my family situation and advised me to work hard to get the job, as there are few opportunities in the sport. I was only twenty-five, had little coaching experience, and I wasn't ready to lead, but they hired me anyway. The connection to Gable and my local roots helped me get the head coaching job at such a young age. Of course, I had to let go of the Olympic Dream. It wasn't really too tough a decision. Denial isn't a place where I lived too often. I assessed my situation, let go of my wrestling career, and began to invest in others.

Hofstra is on Long Island, which was close to my hometown. The program needed an overhaul, just like my life. We weren't a good team, but in time, we would be.

Coach Dan Gable holding Jake, Tom holding Jordan, 1995.

In my experience, the process of achieving the goal became joy-filled. Identifying your priceless does that. It keeps us up late and wakes us up early. There's no separation between work and play when we love our craft. I was experiencing that, thanks to this sport.

Despite my immaturity and lack of experience, my work ethic, and no fear of failing elevated me. I took chances, made mistakes, and fell short. I was obsessed with building Hofstra into a national powerhouse. Sometimes I handled things wrong, and sometimes I tried to do too much at once. But I learned and kept working.

Wrestling was my life, and at some point, my god. At twenty-five-years old, I was back home, a head coach, and ready to lead the Hofstra Pride wrestling program.

1. What's your greatest life disappointment up to now?

2. What goal have you fallen short of?

3. Who do you need to become to meet that goal?

4. What happened when you were promoted beyond your abilities?

5. What are you obsessed about? Is that goal worthy of being obsessed about?

CHAPTER 7
WRECKED BY UNCHOSEN
SUFFERING

The path to finding your
true purpose always
begins on your knees

*For God so loved the world, that he gave his only Son,
that whoever believes in him should not perish
but have eternal life.*

—John 3:16 RSV

For more than twenty years, wrestling had my focused
attention.

I was the head coach at Hofstra University, a small
private school in New York. I led great young men, and my
team excelled. Roman Fleszar was a powerful, committed
lightweight, and Eric Schmiesing a leader who grew into a
great middle weight. These along with Ryan Edmundson,
an Indiana transfer, were my first believers. Because of many

others who followed their example, we began to earn and win the respect of the wrestling fan base.

The worst thing that had happened to me up until that point was losing a wrestling match. On the scale of deep suffering, losing a wrestling match would be located someplace low on the suffering threshold.

On the personal side, I was married to a wonderful woman. We had four children, and my life couldn't have been much better. Sure, we had our moments of challenges raising four kids, working full-time jobs, paying the bills, and dealing with life's trials. But overall, things were going well, so I wasn't in a place of deep pain, and I didn't carve out any time to consider whether God did or didn't exist.

I regularly chose to suffer in the wrestling room because I knew the results. Of course, I suffered most for the things I loved deeply. But, excellence also requires us to invest in things we may not deeply love. It's just more sustainable when we love what we pursue.

However, there's another kind of suffering you and I don't choose. A.W. Tozer talked about this type of suffering, "It is doubtful whether God can bless a man greatly until he has hurt him deeply."[3] Deep suffering often has a distinct, poignant effect on our lives. It did for me. The chosen suffering for me was deep, but not deep enough. Maybe I wasn't tough enough to initiate the type of pain that unchosen suffering caused me.

Welcome to unchosen suffering. Unchosen suffering brought me to my knees. It's a pain inflicted upon us by circumstances outside our control. You wouldn't choose this suffering if given the option. It causes deep wounds and ropey scars on your soul. Not every type of unchosen suffering drops us but the one I experienced did. Nothing prepares anyone for this sudden life alteration. It's a jolting, shocking pain.

At thirty-six years old, I found out through personal experience, and it would change the way I thought and the way I walked on this planet.

At 6:30 p.m. on February 16, 2004, we arrived home from the Hofstra wrestling room. My kids and I gave their mother a break and spent the day together. President's Day recognizes the great leaders of our country and gives the kids a day off from school.

What a day it was. Time spent playing with your children ranks among the best type of day—any parent would agree. We goofed off in the Hofstra wrestling room. We laughed and wrestled. We played dodgeball and handball and ran bases from mat to mat. It was a special day I'll never forget.

At six o'clock, we headed home on the Long Island Expressway in my green Ford Explorer. I looked in the rear-view mirror and saw one of my kids, Teague, asleep on his brother's shoulder. I remember thinking how lucky I was to share life with these children. Some car rides weren't this peaceful. But on this particular night, they were tired from a long day of playing.

We got home around 6:30 p.m., and dinner was on the table. I was supposed to be at a Booster Club meeting at 7:00 p.m. that night, but I called the person in charge to excuse myself from the meeting.

My older brother referred to Teague as a rainbow after a warm sun shower. He was unique, kind, athletic, and strong. A brother to three and friend to more, Teague meant so much to so many. At five-years-old, he was the coach's son who went everywhere I went. When I handed somebody a water bottle in between matches or checked on a player during an injury timeout, Teague was at my side. Because he hadn't started school yet, he often traveled with me. We were great friends, and I loved him.

Teague, Fall 2003   *Tom and Teague. Summer 2003*

Teague loved his sister, Mackenzie, and they spent so much time together. They poured buckets of water on the wrestling room mats and created a makeshift slip-and-slide. Teague loved to wrestle with his older brother, Jake, even though he couldn't beat him. I knew wrestling was going to bond them like it bonded my brothers and me. Jordan, the oldest, was the gatekeeper. He was logical and always showed great emotional control. The four of them were growing up fast and leaning on each other.

At dinner that night, we laughed, relaxed, and told stories about our day. After dinner, Teague drew the short straw to shower first. He wasn't happy about that and jumped up from the table and ran away. At five-years-old he was healthy. He had just started his wrestling training, could do ten pull-ups, and run forever. My wife started to chase him, which evolved into a simple game of hide and seek. We all watched and laughed from the table.

As the chase ensued, Teague didn't realize Lyn was hiding around a corner. He'd lost sight of her in the chase. As he darted past her, she scooped him up. At that moment, while still seated at the head of the table, something overwhelmed me. My body was hit with a strange sensation I'd never felt before. I didn't know what it was and shook it off. But I'll never forget it. When Lyn snatched Teague up into her arms,

I noticed his head dangling a bit, but I didn't say anything because moms are baby-carrying experts. The dogs jumped at him as though something was wrong.

Lyn carried him to the back of the house while the rest of us laughed at their antics. Within seconds, she screamed, "He's not breathing!"

I ran to her and noticed Teague was unconscious. I grabbed him and ran to the coffee table in the living room, where I laid him down and checked his pulse, but there was nothing. His eyes were rolled back. Lyn called 9-1-1. I started CPR, pumping his chest and breathing into his mouth. My children begged me to wake Teague up. I tried. I tried so hard.

I kept thinking the ambulance would arrive. It seemed like forever. I thought I heard sirens. I clutched my lifeless son in my arms and ran down the street, trying to meet the ambulance on the way to our house to save precious time. I was wrong. It was a police car on a different call. I ran back to the house and put him back on the table and kept pumping. It took fourteen minutes for the ambulance and EMT's to arrive. But it felt like hours.

I saw the red lights beaming through our bay window, the one that overlooked the driveway beside the coffee table where Teague laid. I noticed the EMT walking up my driveway. Panicked and scared, when the EMTs opened the front door, I screamed, "Where were you? Fourteen minutes have gone by, and you're right around the corner! Where the hell have you been?"

Pure emotion. Unbridled fear. Total disbelief coupled with frantic concern.

It wasn't their fault. I couldn't help but think about how many false alarms these guys have rushed to in their lifetime. To them, it was just another call.

I thought about the things we take for granted in our lives and the promises we believe we're entitled to. At that moment, I learned the only guarantee is that life is a gift. I didn't need or want this lesson, but I was about to learn much more in the days, weeks, and months ahead.

Quickly assessing the situation, the EMTs grabbed him and rushed him into the ambulance. A family friend came to watch our other children while Lyn and I followed the screaming ambulance in our car. Two things happened in the next few moments. First, I called my best friend, my brother, Frank. I told him something happened to Teague, and we were heading to this hospital. Frank agreed to contact Mom, Dad, and the rest of the family.

As I watched through the ambulance window from my car, the second thing happened. My wife and I started to pray. We had never consistently prayed together in the first eleven years of marriage. In the coming days, I would often find myself on my knees in prayer, but not on this night. In this moment, I was chasing the fleeting hope found in the ambulance that raced my son to the hospital.

We reached out to the God I knew was there but hadn't allowed as part of the inner circle of my life. I believed but never fully trusted enough to commit. Sometimes, we never fully commit until the circumstances demand it.

Family and friends gathered with us in the emergency waiting room. My wife and I clung to each other while we watched the door at the end of the long hall. After an hour and a half, the surgeon walked through that door toward us.

Why won't you look up? Please look up!

As the surgeon approached us with sorrow-filled eyes, he said with a sigh, "I'm sorry." All my life, I've lived with the guarantee that children outlive their parents. I was wrong. The unthinkable couldn't be happening.

At that moment, I felt broken, devastated, lost, and shocked. I felt numb and full of despair. Lyn and I headed to our car to drive the ten miles home in silence. One single event brought me to my knees. It was unrelated to wrestling and far more painful than losing a wrestling match or facing an injury. This unchosen suffering was now our cruel reality.

Teague was gone. We left the hospital without him. As my wife and I pulled into our driveway in Hauppauge, New York, our children came running out the front door. The unthinkable had happened. Up until that moment, I'd willed myself to the desired outcome. But unchosen suffering doesn't care about our will. This suffering is rooted in the laws of life on earth. Sometimes no amount of effort can bring about the desired outcome.

Opening the car door, Jake asked me a critical question I couldn't answer. He said, "Where is Teague?" Jake was Teague's wrestling partner and hero. How does a father answer that question from his eight-year-old son?

That question punched me in the chest as my children waited for an answer.

I knew the names of every top recruit and every weakness, strength, and other things about the student-athletes on my team. But the one thing my children needed at that moment was for me to tell them where their five-year-old brother was. He was rushed to the hospital in an ambulance a mere two hours earlier.

Disturbingly, the leader of their home didn't know. I only knew he was gone. How could I tell my children that one of the few people I'd sacrifice my life for would no longer be at my dinner table, in my wrestling room, or in my bed when he was scared? He'd no longer swim in our brand new pool, jump on his trampoline, or swing on the rope swing. Teague wouldn't be his brother's wrestling partner ever again, nor would he play UNO™ with his sister. He wouldn't ride the team bus with his dad or hand out water to the wrestling team when they needed it. He'd never again walk hotel hallways

> "IF YOU UNDERSTAND WHAT IS TO COME, YOU CAN HANDLE ANYTHING HERE."
> TIM KELLER

wearing his sister's much-too-small bathing suit, thinking it was a wrestling singlet. His mom would never snuggle him in her arms. His dad would never kiss his nose at night and tell him how special and loved he was.

In a moment, my life exploded as if hit by a nuclear warhead. Our world had just shattered.

"He's gone. I'm sorry."

That was hardly good enough. But I didn't know how to answer. We huddled together and cried. We hurt together with so much heartache and deep, searing pain. It was constant and relentless, bone-aching pain.

I remember the pain being so deep I wished I never had kids. I never considered I could lose one. The pain was too much, and I wasn't ready for it. Eventually, my journey moved beyond that feeling.

I made it my life's purpose to answer that simple question—*where was Teague?*

My wife and I had to plan the funeral for our healthy five-year-old son, who suddenly left us. We weren't ready for this. No one would be. How do you describe the devastation? How do you help your children understand what happened when you can't?

My ideal life no longer existed.

At the funeral, my uncle, John, asked me the second question I didn't know how to answer. He said, "What's the meaning of life?"

He'd never asked me that question before. Or, with my focus on otherworldly things, maybe I simply never heard it. I couldn't answer that question either. At least, not with any depth. I'd been busy *doing*—working, raising a family, building a team, living. I never slowed down to consider why I was here or what happens when we die.

Though I knew God existed, I didn't have a relationship with Him. Even though I attended the Catholic Church every week as a kid, with everything in my life going so well, I didn't need God. In fact, I didn't even know if I really believed in Him because my thoughts were based on blindly listening to others.

I was about to learn how much I needed Him in this unchosen suffering.

Lyn and I managed our grief and the pain our children felt. So many marriages crumble in these tragic situations, but we sought help for ours—we needed it. We weren't in a good place. Often, parents can't process their grief and the living children are forgotten in the process. A wise psychologist told us our children would manage their grief as we managed ours. We owed it to our children to get our act together. They'd follow our example. It took a while, but we worked *on* it and *through* it. One of the biggest challenges for me was that the only person who truly could relate to my pain was Lyn.

> BLESSED ARE THOSE WHO MOURN, FOR THEY SHALL BE COMFORTED.
> MATTHEW 5:4 NKJV

This unchosen suffering resulted in vision correction. Now, nothing was more important to me than chasing the truth. I was about to discover my new priceless—the answer to these two questions.

In the midst of the deepest pain, I was laser-focused. My life's most significant journey had begun.

1. What is your priceless?

2. Do you have any guarantees in your life? What are they?

3. Have you experienced unchosen suffering? Describe it and how you dealt with it.

4. Where do you turn to find truth when experiencing your deepest pain?

Tom Ryan Family. Left to Right: Jordan, Teague, Jake, Tom, Mackenzie, Lyn. Winter 2003.

Jordan Ryan and Kaitlynne House

Teague was afraid of everything.
Lyn was stretching his comfort zone.
Winter 2002

Jake and Abbie Ryan's Wedding. September 2018

Mackenzie's wedding in San Diego. October 2019. Left to Right: Ty Willis, Mackie Willis, Lyn Ryan, Tom Ryan

Storming the field at OSU win over Michigan, Fall 2018. Tom and Mackie do this at every home game with Michigan.

Lyn, Tom, Kimme, Frank, Melissa, Dad, Jay. Summer 2019

Fundraiser for Autism, 2016. Raising funds for Ethan for Autism Non-Profit. Front: Kimme. Back left to right: Jake, Dad, Tom, Mackie, Jordan, Lyn

CHAPTER 8
EXCHANGING YOUR
PRICELESS

Transformation begins when we start telling ourselves the truth

You never really know how much you really believe anything until its truth or falsehood becomes a matter of life or death to you.

—CS Lewis

Teague's death wrecked us. The darkest cloud overshadowed our home and invaded our hearts.

On the left side of the paper, I wrote, "God." On the other side, I wrote, "no God." In my quest to find the answer to these two questions, I chased truth and planned to accept whatever answers it brought me.

Was there a creator, or are we the result of chance?

I worked from a clean slate, a blank canvas. I attended church as a kid, but that was it. There wasn't a real relationship or a deep connection. I never had a history with God that allowed me to trust Him.

But that would change. I needed answers, and I was on a journey. Until then, my life was too busy to take the time for this type of deep thought. My thoughts were dominated by simple decisions like what workout I was going to do, what I was going to eat, what event I was going to take my kids to, what car I was going to get next, or what needed to be fixed in the house.

I guess I'd decided years earlier that I didn't need Him because I managed well on my own. In essence, I was the ruler of my kingdom. What I said went. Unchosen suffering changed that.

But now, I wasn't sure what I believed. It was my priceless to get an answer. This priceless became so important that life couldn't move forward without knowing. It was my singular focus, and it entirely occupied my time.

The nagging doubt drove a new hunger to find the truth. I began to read books like Lee Strobel's *The Case for Christ* and *The Case for Faith*. Lee's writings stirred my mind and spirit. He was a brilliant Yale law school graduate and writer for the *Chicago Tribune*, and his journey resonated with me as did his writing and how he processed his faith. What would cause a brilliant person with no faith to move to a place of complete submission and commitment? In the silence of my bedroom, deeply convicted, I turned the pages of his books.

Five main points led me toward God.

1. There's so much historical evidence on Jesus' life and death. No one debates that He was crucified under Pontius Pilate.

2. There's factual evidence of Jesus' burial and resurrection.

3. The fact that the origin of space, time, energy, and matter isn't random. Even the top scientists believe the Universe has a designer.

4. I read and witnessed how prayer can transform people's lives. Even the heart of those who are skeptics can be changed by reading about Jesus and praying.

5. The disciples existed, turned their backs on Him, and later suffered and died for their beliefs. What caused a transformation in them that moved from pretending they didn't know Him to die for Him? They moved from not even believing to a full commitment to Him.

I learned and applied common sense along the journey.

I cried endless tears. I was starved for knowledge about how to understand this life and if there was a next life. I also read *It's Not About Me* by Max Lucado and *The Purpose Driven Life* by Rick Warren. When I returned to work, I listened to audiobooks on the thirty-five-minute daily commute. With pain as my catalyst, I used every free second to gather information.

Charles Stanley's powerful audio teachings made me consider things I hadn't before. His teaching made sense. There was so much love in Scripture and Jesus' virtuous example. I hungered to find the answer to these plaguing questions. I learned my worldview was more narrow-minded than I realized. How could I have lived for thirty-six years and not settled some of these thoughts? Had life been too easy for me up to that point?

Other men and women had searched for these answers, so I decided to learn from them and tap into their expertise and knowledge. Brilliant minds

> GOOD LEADERS CULTIVATE HONEST SPEECH; THEY LOVE ADVISORS WHO CAN TELL THEM THE TRUTH.
> PROVERBS 16:13
> THE MESSAGE

wrestled with this topic and dedicated their entire lives to it. Scientists, world-renowned attorneys, doctors, genetic specialists, and others who'd suffered had all settled the critical question: Chance or Divinity. One side is right—one side wrong. We get to pick. This fact galvanized my mind. Both sides can't be correct. Therefore, I had a decision to make just like every person. I was determined to get to a place where I had enough information to choose.

What did they discover that I didn't know? I pursued this knowledge with every fiber of my being.

A friend of mine encouraged me to read the Gospel of John, which is where I fell in love with Jesus. The Apostle John knew him well. If we want to find out more about someone who has passed, we go directly to their closest friends. John was one of those people in Jesus' life. During the same time, I watched DVD after DVD on evolution. In this massive gathering-of-information phase, my two-sided list began to grow long with facts. It's hard for me to believe anyone can deeply believe in anything or have an opinion if they haven't researched and processed through the facts. I learned about macro and microevolution and kept learning and processing.

Through my tears and research, Jesus became real. At first, it was because I wanted to go to heaven to be with Teague. However, the more I studied Jesus' life, the more my love grew along with my certainty that Teague was with Jesus. And that's where I wanted to be too. There were too many holes in the evolutionary process to believe in chance. I found that believing in chance took more faith than believing in God.

It's not ironic that even my initial decision to move toward Jesus was selfish—it was still about me and what I wanted and needed.

But God meets us where we are. He understood my wounded father's heart. God the Father allowed His Son, Jesus, to die on the cross to fulfill the redemption plan from eternity past. Don't believe for one second that God didn't know my pain. He did. He does. Yet, it's in His redemptive plan through Jesus and His resurrection that I found the answer to every question. There's no way I would've sacrificed my son for anyone. In fact, I would've gladly taken his place, suffering the most brutal death so Teague could live. I would've signed up for that option in an instant. But it wasn't an option.

In my search, I encountered several key questions. Thankfully, through in-depth exploration, I discovered answers to each one of these questions.

KEY QUESTION #1: WHERE IS TEAGUE?

He's fully alive in heaven with Jesus. As D.L. Moody said,

> *Someday you will read in the papers, 'D. L. Moody of East Northfield is dead.' Don't you believe a word of it! At that moment I shall be more alive than I am now; I shall have gone up higher, that is all, out of this old clay tenement into a house that is immortal—a body that death cannot touch, that sin cannot taint; a body fashioned like unto His glorious body . . . That which is born of the flesh may die. That which is born of the Spirit will live forever.* [4]

I now believe this to be true. So many facts pointed me toward this truth. Often, people said, "Well, you needed that to manage your pain." Sure, I was hurting. But my emotions didn't move me in this direction, common sense did. Facts did. Truth did. With the gift of time to reflect and search, I have no doubt that God lifted me and the entire situation. There's no better explanation.

My son lives on the other side of eternity, and someday I'll live with him there, which answered another question. Yes, I'll see him again.

Key Question #2: Who am I?

Isn't this the question in every heart? Doesn't your soul cry with mine to find the meaning of life? I've seen how the world wants us to be defined by its unstable, constantly changing, self-evaluating, whatever-feels-best-in-the-moment, view. Then, we learn how Jesus wants us to see ourselves.

As I read the Gospel of John, I saw that God created me to love and serve Him. He gave me a purpose. God's desire is for me to seek an intimate relationship with Him above all else. He isn't concerned about what I do for Him as much as He is about me living life with Him.

Looking back on my life to this point, I saw His hand leading and directing me. He allowed me to make the choice to pursue wrestling, knowing the disciplines I learned under Coach Dan Gable would provide the framework to seek Jesus. Just as I learned to hunger for growth as a wrestler, now I hungered for something more priceless—truth, identity, the meaning of all life.

> THERE IS A WAY WHICH SEEMS RIGHT TO A MAN, BUT ITS END IS THE WAY OF DEATH.
> PROVERBS 16:25 NASB

In my reflection, I remembered all of those who shared with me along my journey. There was a barber on Wellwood Avenue in New York who re-opened his store after closing to give me a haircut. He shared about God.

There was the priest on an empty bus who chose to sit next to me and talk about his faith. Coach Lenny Zalesky, Barry Davis, and so many poured into me. All those times, I wasn't open enough to deeply process any of their words. Suffering's gifts brought me to this place of openness.

The more I sought Jesus, the more I realized He was worthy of my love. I wanted to follow Him. My pursuit transitioned from simply getting to heaven to walking daily with Jesus. It became more about Him and less about me. That's when

I realized there are only two options for this life and where I'm headed.

KEY QUESTION #3: DOES LIFE CONSIST BY CHANCE?

The first option is chance. Joseph Campbell espoused, "God is a metaphor for that which transcends all levels of intellectual thought."[5] As I evaluated my growing understanding of Jesus, His life, death, and resurrection, the question became, "Was this true? Or, was everything that happened in life purely chance?"

Perhaps a better question comes from Lee Strobel: "We have to ask, 'Why is there no other first-century Jew who has millions of followers today? Why isn't there a John the Baptist movement? Why, of all first-century figures, including the Roman emperors, is Jesus still worshiped today, while the others have crumbled into the dust of history?'"[66]

If everything that happens is by chance, then Strobel's question haunted me. Why is Jesus still worshiped today? If God is a metaphor, as Campbell said, then He isn't present nor does He care about my life.

KEY QUESTION #4: IS THERE A DIVINE CREATOR?

Through my study, I discovered the scientific and overwhelming extra-biblical evidence for the veracity of Jesus' life. In *The Case for Christ*, Strobel writes:

> *Over and over Lapides would come upon prophecies in the Old Testament—more than four dozen major predictions in all. Isaiah revealed the manner of the Messiah's birth (of a virgin); Micah pinpointed the place of his birth (Bethlehem); Genesis and Jeremiah specified his ancestry (a descendent of*

*Abraham, Isaac, and Jacob, from the tribe of Judah, the house
of David); the Psalms foretold his betrayal, his accusation by
false witnesses, his manner of death (pierced in the hands
and feet, although crucifixion hadn't been invented yet), and
his resurrection (he would not decay but would ascend on
high)...* [77]

Through my morning Bible studies with Greg Trunz, and
a pastor, I grew, studied, and listened, and tried to make sense
of this unchosen suffering. The more I studied Jesus' life, the
more I yearned to know and be in a relationship with Him.
My concentrated search for truth heightened my desire for this
salvation He promised. I was lost and knew I needed someone
greater than myself to bring meaning to my life.

In the Gospel of John, there's an interesting discussion
between a Pharisee named Nicodemus and Jesus:

*For God so loved the world that he gave his one and only
Son, that whoever believes in him shall not perish but have
eternal life. For God did not send his Son into the world to
condemn the world, but to save the world through him.
Whoever believes in him is not condemned, but whoever does
not believe stands condemned already because they have not
believed in the name of God's one and only Son.* [8]

I wanted this eternal life with every fiber of my being. This
was my journey to become all God created for me. Chance
began to make little sense the more I dug. My continued
pursuit revealed that God is real, active, and desires a relationship with me.

For the first time, my extreme priceless became my faith
in Jesus. Once wrestling was my God; now my God was
greater—My Creator, Savior, and Redeemer.

Throughout life, we make choices that can be large or
insignificant. Some decisions impact others, and some choices

are personal. I wrestled through my blind spot and saw how God had allowed me to live for thirty-five years with my determination that He was real but not involved in my life. He never forced me to follow Him. True love can only be true love if it has a choice to opt-in or not. He allows us to opt-in, despite having the power to make us love Him. Yet, He gave evidence of His love for me.

He was always there, waiting for me to turn toward Him, and grasp His extended hand. God grieved and suffered with me.

The grief wasn't an easy fix. It was an unwelcome intruder who wrecked our family. Lyn and I grieved the same loss, yet we processed that grief differently. There was no one else on the planet who understood my feelings better than my wife, and I hers. As strange as it sounds, this grief eventually united us.

Don't get me wrong. It was a difficult time for us and our family and still is. There's a hole in our family that'll never be filled this side of eternity. But the more I sought to understand Jesus, the closer I drew to Lyn. Together, we were stronger and more able to support and care for our children, who grieved as well.

At some point in our grief process, how Teague died became a blessing. Since losing Teague, we've learned of other parents whose children died from lengthy illnesses, in combat, through drug addiction, car accidents, or other difficult circumstances. It gave us a new perspective on our unchosen suffering that forced me to seek the truth. Teague died peacefully, the way I would've pleaded for him to if I had a choice. Others have suffered a far more agonizing death.

C.S. Lewis, one of the greatest apologists, also wrestled with understanding suffering as it relates to a loving God. Lewis said, "The problem of reconciling human suffering with the existence of God who loves, is only insoluble so long as we attach a trivial meaning to the word 'love' and look on things as if man were the centre of them."[9]

His statement made sense to me. An Elite wrestler understands that pain is a necessary part of training, gaining strength, and becoming more. I knew this chosen suffering to be good. I welcomed it and sought it out. To get results, you have to go deep. You must harness the power of your mind to become Elite and never relinquish it.

So, why, then, would I believe that unchosen suffering was unfair or not for my ultimate good? Perhaps, this unchosen suffering, like chosen suffering, had a greater purpose.

Faced with these discoveries, I chose the only option that made logical sense—God is real and involved in my life. My definition of love needed to change.

BECOMING ELITE: DATE:

1. Do you know your blind spot(s)? If so, what is it?

2. What are your "I believe" statements? List them.

3. What truths do you long to discover the answers to, and why are these important?

4. Which option do you choose: life without God or life with God? Explain your answer.

CHAPTER 9
EXCELLENCE

Excellence isn't granted at birth; it's a relentless pursuit of your best

As iron sharpens iron, so a friend sharpens a friend.

—Proverbs 27:17 NLT

Becoming Elite is a choice, not a birthright. People aren't born Elite. They must develop traits. I define these traits with the word E.L.I.T.E. For the next five chapters, I'll share my philosophy of what becoming Elite entails.

TRAIT #1: EXCELLENCE

The upper ten percent of any sport is more process-focused than outcome-focused. They fall in love with their suffering and train themselves to zero in on what they can control instead of what they can't. They're the CEOs of their lives.

When no one is watching, they apply the principles of success. They don't need to be led and continuously corrected.

They value the right things and are careful not to fall in love social media reactions and outside opinions. Those focused on Elite-ness exhibit enormous emotional control and master their impulses.

Winning is never something we can completely control. There'll always be the possibility of not winning. Those who suffer the greatest do so because of their deep love of what they're doing. Those who sincerely love what they do can't see the difference between work and play. They're the same. Though some elite people aren't deeply in love with their work, the most sustainable growth occurs when true love is your foundation.

Earning a starting spot on the University of Iowa wrestling team was one of the hardest things I've ever done. As I reflect on that time, it's difficult to explain how much I poured into the sport. In retrospect, it was an endless amount of chosen suffering with doses of other Elite traits.

Though Coach Gable's standards were incredibly high, it never seemed hard in the middle of it. The training gave me a state of bliss because I connect difficult things with blessing. It calmed me and brought me happiness. My desire to make something of my wrestling career mattered. I had come up short so many times before. I had to keep working. Over and over, I saw how deep suffering moved good to great.

Coach Gable never set team goals with us. The only goal was to wake up tomorrow and be better than you were today. We didn't talk about winning championships, but we all knew that any season without an NCAA team title wasn't a successful season. No excuses. Words mattered little. Actions ruled.

We didn't compare ourselves to others. My value was never measured relative to any teammate's value. The only comparison that mattered was to assess how close I was to my maximum capabilities. In essence, was I reaching my full potential?

I was a walk-on, not a recruited team member. It would've been easy to allow my mind to devalue my capabilities and value. The Elite don't think that way. For the Elite, it's not a matter of entitlement. It's a mindset. They self-assess and act on the areas they need to improve.

I chose to be part of the Iowa Wrestling team and received all the amazing perks of being in that program. Often, I thanked Coach Gable at the end of practice for the tough training. I never viewed myself as less than another, and I loved to see my teammates dominate their opponents. I was truly happy for them. They all tried so hard and suffered so much. Quite a few of them won NCAA titles.

Despite never winning one, it'd make little sense to try to discredit anyone else's. That mindset is toxic. Resenting others who attain great things steals our inner potential and pollutes our minds. That trait darkens us from the inside out. As a coach and leader, I won't be around it nor do I allow it around me in any way. Despite my deeply competitive nature, I love watching people attain great things whether they're on my team or not because I understand how suffering works. There is no excellence without it.

When things got tough, I didn't think of myself as a walk-on or believe the team didn't count on me. The only score I kept related to my effort, commitment, actions, desires, and passion for being Elite.

Elite people understand the power of a healthy mindset. Never allow another's opinion to affect your belief. I learned this lesson early in my life. My home life was filled with positive people who valued me for me more than for what I could do. For many people, a scholarship means value. In high school, the scholarship and associated money attached to it mattered. However, after my second year of college, it meant much less. Money wasn't my priceless, being my best was. I'm not implying that everyone should leave a full scholarship behind and inundate themselves with debt to chase a dream.

I'm suggesting that while finances should be a factor in any decision, they shouldn't ever be above placing yourself in the best learning environment.

Understanding this priceless made it easy to leave the money behind and replace it with opportunity. I didn't need Dan Gable to believe in me or tell me I had value to help his wrestling team. I didn't need him to praise me. Sure, it was nice, but I didn't need it. That sense of value in our lives must be built from the inside out rather than from the outside in. My view on life now has only increased this perception. During my first six months at Iowa, Coach Gable rarely spoke to me. It didn't bother me a bit. I knew he cared about me by his actions. When I was my best, my mind was focused on the task at hand. I worked on my mindset and on the things that were in my control.

My self-improvement happened over time. In my first ninety days, I made substantial strides. These days included three practices a day, six days a week. To think we'll attain great things overnight is preloading our minds with the wrong things. Anything worth having requires suffering. Because wrestling is a one-on-one sport, it offers real-time data. Feedback and self-assessment are non-negotiable elements of growth. Every workout allows you to identify critical components that need to improve.

When the brain overloads with concerns about winning or any thoughts that eliminate our control, the body doesn't react as quickly in pressure situations. It's physiological. In most sports, you have a split second to make the proper corrective measures. If the brain has too much going on, the appropriate signals aren't sent to the muscles fast enough.

Therefore, it's critical to train our minds through repetition to control what we can. In wrestling, we practice our attack rate, effort, body language, hand movements, and body position. By doing these processes, again and again, our odds to achieve the desired outcome increases.

In our world, peer pressures, social media, and human influences often flood our brains. But the mindset battle must be won. Preparation always determines the result. Once the contest begins, the training is done, and the perfect execution makes the difference.

I've coached two student-athletes who've won World titles and many who won NCAA titles and earned All-American honors. There was so much to learn from them. Each of them was process-driven. Winning wasn't their primary focus. Controlling what they could was their main focus. They did the right things consistently. They learned feelings can't always be trusted. The mind must keep feelings in balance. This is critically important. Our emotions often speak the easy way into our minds and whispers to us that we're tired and don't feel well. These emotions play on our psyche. Basing any decision in life on mere feelings is a recipe for a mess.

We must understand we aren't always going to be in the mood to train hard, study hard, be there for a friend, or listen to our spouse. It's in these situations where the mind must become the dominant force. We must combat our selfish nature. It's paramount to do what's needed. Living on impulse without discipline gets us nowhere. Following your feelings can be a recipe for a disaster. If we obey our emotions without applying our minds, we'll find ourselves living in a world filled with regret.

Nearly every Elite person who experiences sustained success has great emotional control. This is the ability to resist impulse. This applies on the mat, the field, the court, and in life. I haven't always done this, and it's caused heartache in my life.

In 2013, Logan Stieber was chasing his second straight NCAA title. During the NCAA final match, he was caught in a position that could've resulted in four points for his opponent and changed the match's trajectory. The refs stopped the match to video review the call.

As Logan waited for the outcome of the call, he appeared calm and relaxed. However, as his coach, I was more concerned. The call ended up going our way, and no points were awarded for the position. After the match, I asked Logan what he was thinking during the review. He calmly said, "I quickly did the math in my head, figured out what the score would be, and was ready for either outcome." That's Elite. That's the mindset that allows us to compete freely. It's dispensing the perfect amount of realism into the scenario. Logan didn't allow his mind to unravel. He maintained emotional control.

Logan went on to win that match and two more NCAA titles becoming only the fourth wrestler in USA history to accomplish that feat. A year after graduation, he also won a World title. His calm demeanor, emotional control, and the ability to control his impulses were huge factors in his success. He simply dealt with the truth in every situation. I've seen this quality trait in him expressed as coach, friend, spouse, and leader.

Logan Stieber live in Sports Center after winning his fourth consecutive NCAA Title and leading Ohio State to their first NCAA team title. March 2015.

I could list example after example of how powerful this behavior is in one's life. This isn't something you're born with. It's developed. Staying calm during chaos is a learned behavior and has to be a deliberate choice. You can't be Elite without it.

Chosen suffering requires a focus on preparation. Aggression matters and develops faster than remaining passive. Pain must be part of development. That's why being around high-level people is so critical. Elite attracts the Elite. Elite challenge themselves. They live in a world of truths, and in return, they attract others who want the same things. It's a law of physics. Mass attracts mass. We should continuously ask ourselves what kind of mass we're building because we attract who we are rather than what we want.

Physical preparation is non-negotiable. We must attend to essential components such as skill, cardiovascular, nutritional, rehabilitative, strength, flexibility, power, and speed. Part of the preparation involves trust. Trust precedes all growth because progress stalls without trust. These two elements must work together.

Each of us must face the person in the mirror. It's hard for deep belief and perfect execution to occur without consistent and deliberate preparation. Imperfect preparation doesn't seal our fate. But every great performance relies on solid training. Complete faith in a good plan produces more results than a perfect plan shadowed with doubted outcomes. I love the saying, "A man cannot be fearful and grateful in the same moment." True gratitude is a powerful gift. It's a choice to accept it or ignore not. The opposite of gratitude is entitlement. I've rarely coached anyone to the Elite level who hasn't been grateful.

Gratitude comes from the underlying belief that one's life is no accident. We're here for a purpose and a plan, and there's a power greater than us. Transformation begins with this understanding. When we can't find the answers in this world, where do we turn? The word "gratitude" is a noun, but it has an action component to it. It's not only feeling thankful, but it's also the readiness to express that thankfulness.

Although the Elite love to compete for themselves, a deeper growth occurs when they move toward a higher power. I wholeheartedly believe this saying: "We are not human beings on a spiritual journey, but spiritual beings on a human journey." Our spiritual life should guide us. In nearly every example of an Elite performer, I see an intense spiritual foundation.

A God-centered life is powerful. I've witnessed it over and over again. The testimony in the lives of those who believe is real. One of the most persuasive facts that lead people toward God is the real-life testimony in the transformation that occurs as they pursue Him and begin to live a life that aligns with His way.

It's the relinquishing of our way and submission to His way that leads to our refinement. This constant process of shedding our old self and becoming more like God is never ending. It's an ongoing process that leads to our best self.

Our daily habits ultimately determine how high we'll climb. Habits are repeated actions over time. I've never coached or been around an Elite individual who practiced bad habits. The Elite figure out what needs to get done, and they do it. They don't have to be told or spoon-fed. They just do it. Habits are at the core of the Elite.

An Elite person connects their desires to the required actions and rarely wavers. Many people in the world establish their wants, but they don't consistently practice the habits to bring their desires to complete fruition. An Elite individual understands that sustained success is the result of repeated good decisions over time.

I've coached many who verbalize what they want, yet their actions fall far short. This isn't kid's stuff. It's real-life, tough stuff. We classify this type of behavior as an integrity gap. These gaps must be closed. The Elite don't speak or think of excuses. They problem-solve. They are their best coach. They meet their desires with hard work and relentless action. It's easy to recognize this type of Elite excellence.

Falling short is painful, but pain is a gift. We waste our pain when we don't learn from our losses and discomfort. There are few things in life more devastating than wasted pain. We don't learn from our losses until something is done to correct the problems. That's a tough but true lesson. Failure has the potential to transcend our lives and become a tremendous gift. Every person fails, but what's more important is how we each manage that hurt. The Elite assess, plan, act, and repeat until they're refined.

The Elite use this transformation to create a more specific, almost predetermined outcome. Of course, we don't completely control winning and never will, but a strong plan and solid execution will increase our odds for the desired outcome. A loss drives deeper introspection than a win. It's pain. No one likes pain, but most of us appreciate the learning that comes from it.

Every NCAA, World, or Olympic champ I've worked with experiences deep pain. They fall short of their goal at some point in their careers. In every case, each of them made adjustments. They looked deeper, assessed harder, and planned better. Only a fool experiences pain without making a change.

The Elite grow quickly. They don't wait around for a coach to explain what happened and how to improve. They don't just talk about it. They do it.

I remember J Jagger's frustration during his senior year in college. He was the reigning NCAA champ at 141 pounds, and his senior campaign got off to a tough start. I believe his record was like 7-6 at one point. The wrestling world counted him out by mid-season, but I didn't, and neither did anyone close to him. He had an Elite mindset. He loved to compete and loved the sport. I saw what the world didn't see. He learned lessons from each loss. He identified the underlying issue in most of his defeats—he had an energy problem.

College rules require student-athletes to weigh in one hour before their competition. This becomes extremely tough when cutting weight and dealing with dehydration. J struggled in his matches because he didn't have the energy needed to execute precisely throughout the match. Despite his early-season struggles, I believed he'd correct the issue.

Every morning, I saw him inflict more pain on himself during practice. He exhibited chosen suffering on a daily basis. J's desire to win his second consecutive NCAA title overshadowed any obstacle. So many want to excel on their terms, but few are willing to follow the required blueprint. J's exerted incredible daily effort regardless of his struggles. His actions led him to his desired end goal. By the time the NCAA tournament came, he had paid the price and won his second consecutive NCAA title. He never allowed a loss to define him. Instead, he kept working.

J. Jaggers won 2 NCAA titles in 2008 & 2009. He is one of five in Ohio State history to win more than one. His first title was won with a severe injury late in the match. His best attributes were high intelligence, deep love for the sport, flexibility and extensive chosen suffering.

Failure is a gift. Harness it. Hold onto it. When pursuing your best, failure is your friend. Change happens with action. J was *hard* on himself but never got *down* on himself. There's a difference. We should all walk that tightrope. Harden oneself, but never get down on oneself.

Excellence is the ability to do the work every single time, no matter who's watching. Typically, a small percentage of any team in any organization is willing to do this. Most people aren't willing to give at the required level to get what they want.

For example, Lance Palmer's chosen suffering began when he was just a boy. His father, Dwayne, understood the value of being put under duress. He poured into Lance an incredible work ethic and developed within a competitive spirit. The result of this chosen suffering is not debatable. He won four high school titles, the nation's number one recruit, a four-time All-American, Big Ten outstanding wrestler, and an NCAA finalist. He continued to pursue pain after his college career, which led him to become a two-time world champion in the professional fight league.

Tom with Lance Palmer who was honored at a home dual. Hall of Fame inductee, 2-time PFLMMA World Champion, 4-time All-American, Big Ten Outstanding Wrestler.

Lance Palmer is Elite, along with another wrestler named Mike Pucillo. Both grew up in Northeast Ohio, a wrestling hotbed. Going into his junior year, Mike Pucillo was an elite wrestler and the reigning NCAA champion. Just a week away from the NCAA's, using a box cutter, Mike nearly cut off all his fingers on his left hand. This was his lead hand, the one with which he grabbed his opponent and he used to control his competition. With all the tendons cut through in his hand, when his brain told his hand to close, it couldn't listen. Like the brakes on a bike, squeezing the hand break didn't slow the bike down. The line connecting the hand break to the tire was severed.

At the 2008 NCAA Championships, Sophomore Mike Pucillo defeated Jake Varner in overtime to win at the 184 pound class.

Despite this, Mike was determined to wrestle in the NCAA tournament. He found a doctor who would authorize him to compete. Mike's hand required twenty-three stitches. He had his hand taped closed. With one hand, he made it all the way to the NCAA final again. Mike understood the pain and embraced it. He never once complained or made excuses. That year, 2009, our team finished second in the country. Mike's desire was a big reason why. Excuses weaken us and give up our control. They allow our brain to lose focus and become less solution-focused.

Mike Pucillo finished second in the 2009 NCAA Championships with one hand. Earlier that week, he nearly cut his fingers off. With 23 stitches in his hand to repair it, he couldn't close his fingers.

The Elite pursue excellence. It's non-negotiable for them. As a coach, I don't focus on the Elite. They get it. It doesn't take much to pull them up.

Three-time NCAA championship football coach, Urban Meyer, refers to it as the 10-80-10 rule. Ten percent are Elite, and even when no one is watching, they perform. Eighty percent do the right thing most of the time, which is the compliant group that needs to be lifted into the top ten percent. Finally, the bottom ten percent rarely fall in line and make excuses; it'd be better to remove them.

The largest number of people on any team falls into the compliant group—the eighty percent group. It's the leader's job to move the compliant to the Elite. The compliant group can help the organization the most. The eighty percent must consist of mostly lifters, but the top ten percent must *all* lift. Extending a hand toward another is powerful for both hands connecting.

Unfortunately, most teams have a non-compliant group. They're the excuse-makers who constantly blame others and aren't ever willing to sacrifice for the team. I call these people coach-killers. They take up the majority of the leader's time. More often than not, they waste everyone's time and suck energy from the organization. It never works to hold on to coach-killers. We can only help those who lean into us and want help. Anyone with their back turned toward us isn't reachable. At least not until they turn your way.

The Elite always look your way. They always self-assess. They understand chosen suffering and embrace it. Your biggest challenge as a coach is to get the Elite to pull up the compliant. The most successful organizations in the world understand and live by this truth.

In 2015, I knew we had the talent to win an NCAA Team title, which Ohio State had never done. Winning two team titles as a competitor gave me great insight into what true excellence looked like. I saw it and felt it. I witnessed Elite all around me. I knew we had that in 2015. We also had it in 2008, 2009, 2016, 2017, 2018, and even 2019. We were second in the nation in each of those seasons. In 2015, we won it.

Sometimes, even the perfect plan perfectly executed comes up short. That's always the risk in any organization. We don't control winning. We control preparation. In 2015, we had a loaded team. I don't believe it was as good as the 2018 team, but that team faced a greater obstacle. Our rival in 2018 had five returning NCAA champs. There was only one other team in NCAA history that could claim that.

In 2015, we had the team to win it. To do this, we needed to pull a compliant student-athlete up to the Elite level. Our team had talent up and down the lineup. Our leader, Logan Stieber, was chasing his fourth NCAA title. Only three men in NCAA history had accomplished this feat. Logan was the heavy favorite and ended up winning that year as well becoming the fourth man to win the NCAA title each of his four seasons.

Logan Stieber, from Monroeville, OH, won 4 NCAA titles and a World Championship. The first man on earth to accomplish such a feat. His emotional control, intelligence, deep love for the sport, and constant suffering were his greatest guides.

We also had a few dominant super-freshmen. Bo Jordan was the nation's top overall recruit out of high school. He grew up just sixty miles from campus in a legendary wrestling family. His dad is a Hall of Fame coach who was also a multi-time NCAA All-American. His uncle, Jim, was a two-time NCAA champ who had a few boys who were college stars. Bo won four state titles and was a four-time All-American. Despite his great success, a severe injury hampered him most of his career. He never let the injury control his mindset. He made the necessary adjustments.

Another Elite team member on the 2015 National Championship team was Nathan Tomasello, a freshman, and the nation's top recruit. Nate was a four-time high school state champ with a relentless desire for excellence. Like the other Elite on the team, he shone on the mat and in the classroom. He held himself to the highest standard as well as others around him. Nathan won the National title as a freshman, only one of sixteen men in history to do so.

Incoming freshman Kyle Snyder played a huge role in the 2015 team. As a freshman, he came in with high goals. He was the nation's top overall recruit and made it to the NCAA title match as a true freshman. He scored huge points for this team, and his leadership was strong.

The combination of Nathan Tomasello, Logan Stieber, Bo Jordan, and Kyle Snyder gave us the nucleus we needed to win a team title. I knew this group would get us close, but we had others on the team who weren't Elite-minded, though they were compliant. We needed to lift them. Their help would push the team over the edge.

The Elite are true leaders and encouragers who lift people along their journey. They are other-centered rather than self-centered. They care about the team. In 2015, my team needed to lift, and they did.

A sometimes-compliant, super-talent named Kenny Courts gave us the spark we needed to win in 2015. He was the focus of most of my attention as well as others on my staff. We pushed, pulled, and lifted him. Our strength and conditioning coach, Don Moxley, poured into him as well. The Elite four were business, as usual, all year long. In their four or five years at Ohio State, none of that group ever entered my office for a disciplinary reason. Each wrestler was a four-time Academic All-American who did what the Elite do. Kenny, on the other hand, struggled a bit more. In March of 2015, the team propelled him to the NCAA semi-final, which ensured him All-American honors and the Buckeyes an NCAA team title.

Excellence lifts. It's honest, tough, truthful, resilient, and demanding. It chooses the hard way—chosen suffering. Excellence loves.

The greatest force in the world is positive influence.

1. Who sharpens you? Make a list.

2. What three lessons have you learned from a parent, teacher, or coach? Write them down.

3. Do you pursue chosen suffering? Why or why not?

4. Who are the positive influences in your life? Are you moving toward them or away from them?

5. Are you compliant in any area? Write them down along with the corrective actions to transform these areas into Elite.

Chapter 10
Leadership

Be the CEO of your life; becoming Elite depends upon it

Whoever heeds discipline shows the way to life, but whoever ignores correction leads others astray.

—Proverbs 10:17 NIV

All great leaders are examples of those who embrace pain and suffering while sharing truth in love. The Elite take full ownership of their life and decisions. These are the non-negotiables of leadership.

My summers spent at the J Robinson wrestling camps exposed me to physical abilities I didn't think were possible. In one month, I received the physical, mental, and emotional training of an entire high school season. The environment connected me to other like-minded students who pushed me to be my best. When I went home after those camps, I sought others I could challenge and who'd challenge me.

TRAIT #2: LEADERSHIP

People cannot lead others any higher than they're willing to drive themselves. To be a great leader, you must carefully and honestly examine your life. Only when we're willing to look in the mirror, do we gain the wisdom needed to assess our situation. It's easy to ignore our shortcomings. Good leaders practice regular self-assessment and adjustment. *Great* leaders invite others to speak the truth grounded in love into their lives. When that happens, truth promotes growth.

Coach Gable masterfully taught us to choose duress—the ability to physically and mentally push beyond your current limits. I'm convinced my time at Iowa opened doors for me in life that wouldn't have been possible otherwise. Getting hired at Hofstra was a dream. Having spent four years at Iowa immersed in one of the most intense, competitive cultures in the sport, and then two years as the assistant coach at Indiana, I was ready to roll up my sleeves and bring pride to Long Island through wrestling.

My wife and I packed up the truck, our two sons, Jordan and Jake, and headed back to New York where we'd be close to family and familiar surroundings. We were starting our life together. I'd grown up eight miles from Hofstra and had trained in that wrestling room. It was 1996, and we were full of optimism.

Anything that has any value demands much of you. As I began my first year at Hofstra, I faced struggles. This occurs in every organization that succeeds at an Elite level. We have to learn to embrace struggles, hold on to small victories, assess, decide, act, and repeat. I brought with me the many lessons I learned from Coach Gable. His system was deeply rooted in timeless principles. I took his principles and instilled them into the men in the Hofstra program. The system searched for men who hunger, love the sport, and love to do what few are willing to do.

I quickly realized the culture at Hofstra lacked strength. Instead, there was too much doubt and confusion that needed to be eradicated through hard work and consistency. Building a program of national prominence demanded everything. We desperately needed talent, which came through intense recruiting and relationship building. Though there are many building blocks to success, the most potent ones are love and surrounding yourself with the right people. These two feed off each other.

As a leader, I surround myself with the right type of other leaders. I empower these leaders to make decisions. True leaders want to make a difference. If we don't allow them a voice, we ultimately lose them and compromise our organization. A motto we, The Ohio State Wrestling coaching staff, live by is the depth of any organization is defined not by who gets the credit but rather by the deep commitment of all involved. Great teams and organizations are birthed when no one cares who gets the credit.

People love to be around a big vision, feel valued, and believed. They hunger for purpose and the desire to feel needed. Great leaders share and embody this. Great leaders are deep thinkers and humble. Organizations shrivel when the leader is unable to look inward rather than outward. Outward focus is easier than inward focus. Inward focus transforms. The most toxic environments in the world lie buried under our skin. When we don't utilize our free will to cleanse the toxicity, we damage the team we lead.

That first year as head coach at Hofstra was tough. We had a cap of nineteen people who weren't ready for this level of competition at the time. We lost every single match in the first round of the conference tournament. No one won. At the end of the tournament, I walked under the bleachers and broke down.

After that first season, I did an overall assessment of the program. The two main areas that sustain and lift an organization from weak to powerful are recruitment and development. I skipped the NCAA tournament that year and went on a recruiting campaign. It turns out that it was a smart decision as we landed a few commitments from men who had the talent to compete at this level. More importantly, they embodied the deep desire and work ethic necessary to build a championship team. They understood chosen suffering would be the foundation of our rise.

The athletic department at Hofstra couldn't afford to fund us as well as some of the programs with big departments and a massive donor base. That didn't bother me because I knew it up front, but it created recruiting challenges with scholarship dollars that were one-third of the allowance for private schools. Therefore, we focused on what we could control—vision, passion, and love. We worked hard. When I was hired, I had a part-time assistant under the NCAA allowances for a team like ours. Over time, I got one full-time assistant when other programs had two full-time assistants.

When building, growing, and strengthening your leadership team, meet regularly. Always listen to their input and concerns. Have engaged communication with your fellow coaches but also with your student-athletes. When needed, take swift action. Hire and recruit for character, then water it and allow it to flourish.

As the coach at Hofstra, we built a wrestling program. It could've been a company selling widgets. It doesn't matter. There are similarities when building any organization. Success leaves clues too. Find a leader who loves people and loves his craft. This leader must live in truth via deep, internal inspection. If the leader does all this and has a clear vision, over time, a sustainable, successful organization emerges.

It's always about sacrifice. To gain something, we must trade something for it. Often, it's our time and comfort. Don't get me wrong—competence, character, and connection matter. These are the three C's for leading anyone.

However, it starts with a genuine love for the sport and the people in it. People made the Hofstra program, not me. Life isn't about me. Building something great isn't a *me* thing. It's always an *us* thing.

The actions of a few inspire many. Roman Fleszar, a powerful, explosive driven prospect from New Jersey, and Eric Schmiesing, a tough, hard-working farm boy from Minnesota, were two of the earliest Hofstra believers. I refer to these two as the apostles of Hofstra's rebuild to prominence. These two along with Ryan Edmundson, a transfer from Indiana, were great leaders. Ryan is one of the toughest wrestlers I have coached. Injuries sidelined his greatness on the mat, but his work ethic and the manner in which he carried himself was what all the Elite show.

He tore his ACL two times his senior year. Upon returning from his first tear, he won our two-mile pre-season run. Ryan determined to reach his full potential and pursued chosen suffering. Today, he is a state trooper, happily married, and has raised his children to make a difference. Because top recruits like these men committed to the Hofstra program, more of the right people joined on. People matter.

Nationally, many programs experienced years of success. We were different. We were building value. The flood gates opened. Love and passion prevailed. The apostles' success echoed, and men of character and vision came from all over but mainly New York, Pennsylvania, and New Jersey—all hotbeds of wrestling.

I think back to high school standouts like Jason Debruin, Noel Thompson, Joe Rovelli, Rob Anspach, Dennis Papadatos (a determined walk-on and current head coach at Hofstra), Russell Jones, Mike Quaglio, James Strouse, and Joe Catalanotto, who were native New Yorkers and chose Hofstra. Dave Tomassette, Brad Christie, Tom Noto, and Paul Siemon were tough New Jersey boys. All-Americans like Chris Weidman (UFC champ), Mike Patrovich, Chris Skretkowicz,

Jon Masa, Charles Griffin, Russell Jones, and Alton Lucas brought a higher level attainable to Hofstra.

One of my favorites was Ralph Everett, a three-time Florida state champ who came to Hofstra to play football. He was undersized on the football field, at least the coach thought so. Coach asked me to take him off their scholarship roster, but I couldn't do so without spending time with him. I had to live beside him and get to know him, so I invited him to train with our team. A 165-174 pounder, he played linebacker his freshmen year at Hofstra. It didn't take me long to learn what was inside this man. He was smart and had an inner strength coupled with power. After a month of observation, I believed in him, called the football staff, and said, "We want him." During his time at Hofstra, he delivered in many ways. His actions were always right. Eventually, in the second round, he knocked off the reigning NCAA Champ who was the number one seed at the NCAA tournament. More importantly, now he's a successful accountant and father.

Love works. It's hard sometimes, but it's a dynamic in our lives. As the team improved, Hofstra Athletic Director, Harry Royle, gave more love, which ignited *more* success. The increased success brought more fans, which allowed our student-athletes to feel a higher level of respect. Love and respect go viral.

Our new level of success caught the commitment of donors, big and small. Each one mattered. A former high school standout from Westbury who worked hard on the mercantile exchange, Scott Arnel, did well. His boys wrestled at the Elite wrestling school held at Hofstra. Scott became a change agent through a big boost and asking others to also help, like his longtime friend, Lee Spiegel. Former Hofstra head coaches, Tony Arena, Nick Gallo, and Neil Duncan all left to build companies, but they helped as well. My long-time friend, Guy Savia, jumped in too. People made the difference.

Because I wrestled at Iowa, I thought I knew coaching. But I had much to learn as one of the youngest head coaches in the nation. One of those critical lessons is exterminating emotions and impulsive behavior. This is non-negotiable for any Elite person. Any lack of impulse control is destructive. Emotions must be continually addressed and diligently managed. I struggle in this area. When I look back on my life, I identify several periods where my lack of emotional control caused me to make a poor decision that resulted in even more pain for me and those closest to me.

The truth is everyone fails. The better question to ask is why we failed and what we learned from that experience. Are we hungry to learn? It's insane not to learn from every failure. Decisions and actions are like highways heading somewhere. Therefore, we must consider the road we choose, which is a simple but powerful truth. I can predict what lies at the end of every path we choose. The question isn't so much about where the way is leading. That's the easy part. The hard part is to decide to get off the road leading nowhere, and instead, jump on the road heading to somewhere productive. The foundation of this transformation starts within each of us. We must develop our worldview and what it is we truly want.

As an athlete, I trained year after year with men who yearned to achieve the highest standard. It was a cycle of greatness. The tradition continued with new names. This sustained success was under the watchful eye of Dan Gable, multiple NCAA champ and Olympic champ. As a competitor, Gable was known for his relentless work ethic and for overheating his opponents with constant pressure. He was my mentor. His way was proven. Many who wrestled for him moved from college athlete to coach. His success and way have had a ripple effect in the wrestling community through a long lineage of coaches, including me.

1. Look in the mirror and describe the person you see.
   What's your worldview? What are your dreams?
   What are your fears?

2. Who's a truth-teller for you? Who are you a
   truth-teller for?

3. Look back over your success, what were your game
   changers?

4. What kind of leader are you? What identifies you as
   this type of leader?

Chapter 11
Initiative

You solve problems when you're in a heightened state of awareness

Make today a day lived in alignment within, with others, and toward a worthy aim. Live hard. Love harder.

—Chet Scott

Struggle is at the center of all growth. Ache is my favorite word when it comes to learning anything. Nothing comes free—not wisdom, truth, success, or even sadness. Sadness costs. Becoming Elite requires you to go beyond your current ability to push toward your best.

Trait #3: Initiative

It's always going to be hard, so having a growth mindset is critical. Wrestling teaches you how to assess, evaluate, and determine your next best course of action within a moment's time. When in the throes of a match, you don't have time to consult your coach. A good coach has trained you to anticipate and react to situations with intelligent decisions. Using common sense to problem solve is at the core of transformational decision making.

I didn't fully understand the components of coaching when I was hired by Duane Goldman at Indiana University or when I competed for Dan Gable. At least I couldn't verbalize what it meant to be a coach. Even after twenty-seven years of coaching, I still learn every day. The principles of success haven't changed, but there's always learning.

There's a difference between living a life of chosen suffering and forcing it onto others. I believe that coaches are critically important in all of our lives. Whether you're on a sports team or not, all of us need coaching. A coach doesn't need to have a whistle around their neck. We need people who care about us and challenge us to move from where we are to where we want to be. Coaches challenge, encourage, and share truth. They share truth in love. That's what we all want.

At Ohio State University, we've implemented a repeatable training system. Just like the J Robinson camps and the Gable Method, success isn't by chance. We create success and repeat it if done correctly.

When we recruit athletes, we look for natural ability, of course. But more than that, we look for character and that inner fortitude to move beyond natural ability. We look for men who have exhibited a high level of emotional control. We see this in how they win and lose. We hear it when we speak to them. We work diligently to recruit this trait. It's a mindset and a work ethic that's required to be Elite in any area.

Without some natural ability, you won't progress to an Elite level. God gives us different talents. We need to pursue those to their fullest. Just like football didn't make sense for me, not every person who loves wrestling can wrestle for a state title, NCAA title, or Olympic Gold. Sometimes no amount of chosen suffering makes these things possible. That's not the point though. What matters is that we live up to our abilities through chosen suffering. The more you love what you do, the better chance you have.

Natural ability is never enough. That's the challenge for us coaches. Who do we see in high school programs that exhibit signs of mental toughness, intellectual prowess, and moral character? Those who desire to move to the Elite level must have these components present.

At the Ohio State University Wrestling, my vision is to:

- Foster a relentless pursuit of personal growth where love, gratitude, and deep chosen suffering bind us to our purpose and a deeper connection.

- Allow each athlete to grow into his unique self.

- Understand that the whole is always an integral part of the equation.

- Exterminate damaging pride and fear.

- Elevate truth and love.

- Overshadow *me* by *we.*

- Help student-athletes have well defined beliefs, and make steps toward the pursuit of them.

Modeling the way *is* the way. Example is the greatest teacher. Together, we build athletes who love their sport and learn and pursue that which leads to their development as the best version of themselves.

Therefore, we:

- Provide the world's greatest training environment to inspire those whose priceless is to reach their full genetic potential.

- Create the world's best competition environment that moves the spirit of all who attend.

- Build a culture of truth and love—a culture of bold men who communicate genuinely with each other.

- Build a culture whose foundation is on behaviors over rules.

- Build men who value toughness as much as slickness.

- Over-communicate and listen intently.

- Be vulnerable and real.

- Share truth. Always share truth.

IT STARTS WITH UNCONDITIONAL LOVE

Not every athlete experiences unconditional love in their home like I did. Therefore, one of the first things I give my athletes is the knowledge that win or lose, they have my love and support. We work on the weaknesses, techniques, and mental toughness. But like Coach Gable taught me, I don't make a win or loss personal. Their value as a human being is intrinsic, not the result of their effort.

There's nothing more valuable than understanding you matter because you exist, not because of something you do. My parents gifted me with this love, which was later reinforced by the most amazing God. Some athletes don't come to our program with this understanding. So, it's one of the first gifts we impart. We desire to build the individual first. The team is only as strong as the individuals who comprise it.

Jesus embodies unconditional love. The Bible says most people wouldn't be willing to die even for a good person, but Christ died for us because of His love even though we didn't realize the depth of our sin.[10] God loves us absolutely without qualifications. As a dad, I love my children from the moment of their birth. They didn't do anything to deserve my love. It's inherent. I can't stop loving them. My daughter Mackenzie, like every daughter, should feel the deep love from her father and that he is willing to die for her. I would give my life up for her in a moment. Of course, she can also choose to have a savior as well who did do that for her.

To become Elite, the gift of unconditional love is a game-changer. There's enough pressure to succeed without adding performance anxiety. An athlete, business person, leader, or anyone seeking success must define their self-worth intrinsically as a child of God the Creator.

THE THREE C'S OF ELITE-NESS

Competence

Sustained success starts with talents and gifts. But these aren't enough to become Elite. The promise of ten-minute-abs is a farce. It takes ten minutes every day for the next two years to achieve your desired results. Therefore, your work ethic immediately matters.

Here's how I define an Elite work ethic: the ability to repeatedly take yourself into chosen suffering. An athlete who develops this work ethic grasps the truth that Elite-ness comes from absolute love for their desired outcome. It isn't drudgery or coercion. Our athletes choose to surround themselves with truth-tellers and life-givers.

When an athlete enters our program, we start by connecting them with their "seal" buddy. Doing so removes isolation. They have someone who helps them transform their mindset to an Elite one.

The concept of a seal buddy comes from the United States Navy Seal training. As former Navy Seal, Eric Davis says, "Choose your swim buddies: You are who you hang out with." Humans tend to fall in line with their environment. Therefore, those with an Elite mindset tend to stick together and train together. This mindset runs toward the truth, not away from it. According to this model, you don't rise to the occasion—you fall to your training level.

Competency relies on training. You have to know that you've paid the price. Day in and day out, you work on areas that need improvement. You study your opponent, and you understand their tendencies. Most importantly, you know your strength and weaknesses.

Therefore, developing competence first involves learning a new mindset. This focuses on:

1. **How to listen.** Active listening means tuning into the words, emotions, and body language of the person speaking. You aren't waiting for the opportunity to reply or present a rebuttal. Instead, you're able to articulate back to the person what they said.

2. **How to speak and the power of speaking concisely.** Speaking and talking are different. It's important to speak concisely and clearly in every situation and to articulate your thoughts to say exactly what you mean.

3. **How to write.** We ask our athletes to write what they heard and how they feel. It's a powerful discipline to write out your thoughts because it brings clarity.

This process is done in a group setting we call Built to Lead practices, which I learned from my coach, Chet Scott. Our athletes come from all walks of life. They're from different socio-economic backgrounds, weight classes, skin colors, large families, small families, and areas of the country. Through conversation, we work on building an Elite team through honest communication, trust, and lack of judgment. In this way, we bring them into the Ohio State University wrestling family while they're training.

Connection

Sometimes, we have to unravel past behaviors based on previous results. Our goal is to help them develop a deep love for wrestling so their *work* becomes *play*. L.P. Jacks describes this concept like this:

> *A master in the art of living draws no sharp distinction between his work and his play; his labor and his leisure; his mind and his body; his education and his recreation. He hardly knows which is which. He simply pursues his vision of excellence through whatever he is doing and leaves others to determine whether he is working or playing. To himself, he always appears to be doing both.*

If your value has been based on your performance, where dinners were different based on whether you won or lost, our goal is to retrain the athlete's mindset toward controlling their thoughts and preparation. At OSU wrestling, athletes are loved regardless of results.

Character

Character is defined by *who you are*. Reputation is built on *who the world thinks you are*. There is a big difference between these two, and we must close the space between them. Character is built one decision at a time. It's a series of small decisions followed by actions based on the growth mindset necessary for success.

An Elite athlete focuses on small victories. These become the building blocks to develop self-confidence. For instance, for the last month, your Seal buddy got you so tired during warm-ups you could hardly function. But yesterday, after a month of hard training, you were winded but not exhausted. You see how your choice to add an extra hour of running to your training schedule and increasing your nutrition results in greater endurance.

Elite athletes are problem solvers. Our default as humans is abdication. All you have to do is listen to a few conversations to discover that humans say what we want, but we aren't willing to back up with action. Instead, we offer excuses instead of taking responsibility. But that's not the way of the Elite.

In any field, successful people own their decisions and stand by the results. When you're on the mat, you have to quickly evaluate your opponent and your options and decide on your best course of action to win. Remember, as a coach, I'm going to love you no matter the outcome. You hone in on the things you can control, like your thoughts. Keep it simple. Elite athletes can explain their decisions because they made them with complete focus and integrity. Winning isn't something you can control.

Another characteristic that's important for an Elite athlete to develop is self-assessment. You're your greatest coach. Decide that you aren't going to take everything personally. Don't make assumptions. The only thing you can control is how you react to external circumstances. How well do you understand who you are? Are you able to honestly evaluate your decisions, actions, and progress?

How do you treat others? We encourage our athletes to treat others the way they want to be treated, to chase the hard way, and to be the one who seeks forgiveness first. It's easy to serve others when you have a strong foundation in a higher power. Have you grounded yourself, or are you listening to the world and swinging right to left and back again? When I realized that Jesus Christ is God and wanted a relationship with me, I discovered the truth for my existence. This became the bedrock of my life.

WHEN I CONCLUDED THAT JESUS CHRIST IS GOD AND WANTED A RELATIONSHIP WITH ME, I DISCOVERED THE TRUTH FOR MY EXISTENCE. THIS BECAME THE BEDROCK OF MY LIFE.

However good you think you are, someone is better. Therefore, develop true humility. Respect those who reveal your weak areas. They've given you a gift in the opportunity to improve in that area of your life. Choose each day to work alongside others who push you to greater levels of suffering. It's one of the things I love about sports.

Leaders set the example. Therefore, it's imperative to focus on self-improvement. What books do you love? What information do you consume to improve as an individual?

Self-assessment always builds mental and physical endurance. An athlete who chooses this way has enough love and passion for pursuing the highest levels of success. They've set aside the distractions and the negative influences as much as possible, to press into their priceless. An Elite athlete at this level routinely chooses to suffer out of love for the outcome. They visualize their goal clearly and realistically. Every step along the path is attainable because they've assessed the necessary components to achieve it.

When I see athletes move into this level of character development, I'm ecstatic. These are the leaders for others on the team to follow. In many respects, they become coaches to the younger athletes in our program.

Human beings want things to go well. But unchosen suffering causes the most growth. An Elite person understands the value of both chosen and unchosen suffering and wholeheartedly pursues the ache.

This process is a constant cycle of rinse and repeat. What you fill your brain with you move toward. Decide what to put down and when.

BECOMING ELITE: DATE:

1. On a scale of one to five, rate your initiative.

2. Do you have a growth mindset? What evidence backs up your answer?

3. Which of the Three C's of Elite-ness is your weakest?

4. To improve your Elite-ness, what will you change, adopt, or practice starting today?

CHAPTER 12
TEAMWORK

The size of your fight is directly proportionate to the depth of your love

All joy reminds. It is never a possession, always a desire for something long ago or further away or still about to be.

—CS Lewis

March of 2015 was a historic moment for Ohio State wrestling. We hoisted the National Championship trophy high above our heads. After finishing second in 2008 and 2009, this title felt good.

TRAIT #4: TEAMWORK

Happiness is a feeling that comes and goes with our circumstances. Joy is something far greater.

I came to this deeper understanding in 2004, eleven years earlier. The sudden and tragic death of my five-year-old son caused the transformation. Through my intensive pursuit of truth, my space had been filled. No number of trophies is big enough to fill a person's empty space. Only one thing can fill that space that each of us has. Of course, we try to fill it with all sorts of things the world offers us, but each attempt will come up short, time after time.

This NCAA team title was a great accomplishment. It brought so much happiness. We passed the first-place trophy around among team members and staff.

2015 NCAA Championship. Ryan Family Left to Right: Tom, Mackenzie, Jake, Lyn, Jordan

My second son, Jake, stood beside me on the platform. A redshirt, he was Logan Steiber's training partner that year. He hoisted it too. What a moment—father and son celebrating. My oldest son, Jordan, and daughter, Mackenzie, were there beside my wife, Lynette. We were all thrilled.

The trophy was a visual representation of the gifts that the unified sacrifice of a team can bring. So many of us were deeply committed to the very difficult process of crossing over from simply believing. The crowd roared. The Buckeye faithful exploded with an "OH-IO!" So many faces smiled in the arena. Hundreds of thousands of fans watched on ESPN from their homes.

The state of Ohio is filled with families deeply rooted in the sport. Wrestling has the sixth-highest participation among high school athletes. America loves wrestling. It's good for our country and for the world. Wrestling teaches transformational lessons in humility because it's raw and real. There's no hiding, just like in any well-lived life.

The Buckeye Nation was alive, and wrestling was booming in Columbus, Ohio. High school wrestling produces so many wrestling legends. Finally, they had an NCAA title to rejoice over. On air, live, ESPN interviewed one of those legends, Logan Stieber. Earlier that evening, he became the fourth man in NCAA wrestling history to win four NCAA titles. Logan knew how to train. He was hard-working, tough, skilled, and loved his craft. Logan was bred for it and understood chosen suffering.

Though Logan was always stoic, he trusted too. Early in life, he jumped the gap from *believing* to *committing*. Not everyone can commit, but Logan's parents, Jeff and Tina, raised both their boys to respect chosen suffering.

The Steiber family commonly practiced sacrifice in their home. Instead of taking family vacations, they chose to spend their money and time on wrestling camps, clinics, and related travel. Hunter, Logan's younger brother, was a two-time all-American and the heartbeat of this National Championship team. Competing with just one arm, he inspired us all. The city of Monroeville, Ohio, with 1,400 residents, proudly boasts of the two who led the Buckeyes to their first-ever NCAA team title.

The elevated stage in the center of the arena was filled with our team, staff, and administrators. Athletic Director Gene Smith, the man who gave me the opportunity to coach at Ohio State, was part of this history, along with my Sports Administrator, T.J. Shelton. So many quality, hard-working people in our department made a difference. My family is blessed to be a part of the Buckeye Nation. Gene made that decision to bring us here, and the Ryans are forever grateful.

My profession is coaching wrestling. Winning feels good, but it's not my purpose. It's crucial to know the difference.

2015 Big Ten & NCAA Team Champions. First one in The Ohio State history. The Ohio State Team placed second in 2008, 2009, 2017, 2018, 2019. We placed third in 2016.

As the trophy celebration concluded at 10:00 p.m., we felt elated by the endorphins released from giving so much to attain something so meaningful. The Buckeyes were the 2015 NCAA wrestling champions.

There are few things more powerful than a handful of individuals who come together to work alongside each other and accomplish something special. This was the first NCAA Wrestling title for The Ohio State University and only the 12th Division I program in NCAA history to win a team title. Being the first to do something so big is historic and unique. On a high, we enjoyed the fruits of total sacrifice.

Following the trophy's hoisting, the staff and team met roughly 1,000 fans at a post-championship celebration. The energy in the room was electric from the die-hard wrestling fans, Buckeye fans, and supporters who were there to celebrate with us. It was memorable, emotional, and unforgettable. Big and small accomplishments elevate us. They build trust that we're on the right path.

My entire family was by my side while the one not there looked over me—Teague. What a gift to have them all present for this moment. Everyone in the room owned a piece of the trophy. One of the wonders of sports occurred—people from all over the country put away their burdens for a few days and came to give the gift of support to others. Spectators left behind their pains and struggles to focus on others. We were deeply connected, and it felt amazing.

One of our team leaders spoke to the large crowd. His words echoed across the room into the hearts and minds of everyone in attendance. Wrestling legend, Kyle Snyder, a freshman phenom, while up 1-0, was caught and pinned in the NCAA title match. He planned to win four. So many big dreams shattered in that moment. Though he didn't want to speak, he did. He didn't even want to be there as his heart and ours were ripped out just two hours before. Sure, he was happy for the program. Kyle made a difference. But with that sense of pride, he also dealt with his pain.

Kyle, a consummate warrior, went on to prove it. Suffering's gifts pierced him and took him to an even higher sense of focus. He went on to win the next three NCAA titles, two World titles, and an Olympic Gold, all while in college. His combined collegiate and international record is unmatched in USA wrestling history. On this night, however, he fell short. Though suffering, he spoke anyway. "I am heartbroken right now. I am hurting, but if this is the worst thing that ever happens to me, I have lived a blessed life."

An eighteen-year-old just poured wisdom all over the room, and I wasn't a bit surprised. Kyle's clarity in his life allowed him to hold onto something bigger. His internal space was already filled, and no number of trophies could fill what was already packed. He knew his why, and his purpose was clear. The listening crowd stood in awe. In these few sentences, Kyle exemplified the depth of his love for his brothers.

That summer, just a few months after the NCAA final loss, Kyle became a world champion defeating the reigning Olympic Champ for a spot on the USA National team. He was the youngest World Champ in USA wrestling history. Love is a powerful tool. Kyle loved the sport, competing, and his creator. His suffering was rooted in deep love.

Logan, our senior team leader, stood up as well and thanked the crowd. He'd wrestled his last match as a Buckeye. Recognized as the Hodge trophy winner, an award given to the nation's best college wrestler, he's one of the top-five college wrestlers of all time. More men have walked on the moon than have won four NCAA titles. The small-town country boy from Monroeville, OH, in his quiet, gentle voice shared and gave everyone the uplifting moment that heroes do.

Coach Tom Ryan, Nathan Tomasello, Bo Jordan, Kyle Snyder. First three men in NCAA history to become 4-Time All-Americans together. Their leadership and Elite qualities helped lead The Ohio State to our first ever NCAA team title in 2015 and two runner-up finishes (2017 & 2018) and a third place finish (2016).

The rest of the team spoke as well. Super freshman, Nathan Tomasello, became the fifteenth man in history to win an NCAA title as a freshman. A northeast Ohio wrestling legend, Nathan won four state titles in high school. Living up to his high expectations, Nathan went on to win four Big-Ten titles and become a four-time All-American.

Bo Jordan, a high school legend, finished as a freshman All-American and won the title-clinching match for the team. He, too, went on to claim four All-American honors. Senior, Kenny Courts, finally broke through in his senior season to earn All-American honors giving the team a big boost and much-needed points.

The words and actions of our program's leaders mesmerized our fan base. They witnessed history and a culture deeply embedded in love, integrity, hard work, truth, and commitment. Great athletes come and go, but a deep culture sustains. It attracts and produces a harvest that can be reproduced.

It's been said that it's lonely at the top. That isn't the case for the Ohio State program. Not if you do it right. The *top* on that night was filled with so many. The celebration brought much happiness to many lives. So many lifted, gave, cared, and were a part of the family. We laughed and hugged. Some cried out of disappointment. The emotions were all over the place. However, we all grew together.

The morning came fast but was quite different than a few hours earlier. The team bus was set to depart at 6:00 a.m. Unlike a mere six hours ago, it was quiet and peaceful. ESPN, our Ohio State supporters, and the crowd of 20,000 screaming fans were nowhere to be found. Silence filled the air.

The team threw their bags in the storage compartments under the bus and climbed aboard the forty-five-seat passenger bus—no fancy-chartered plane. Many were tired and sore from the three brutal days of competition. Like life, wrestling is hard. All of the cortisol poured out that night, and the morning offered the opposite effect. Some men on the bus accomplished what they came for, while others didn't. However, they all battled.

Of the ten competitors, five were crowned All-Americans, and five weren't. The team won, but not everyone achieved what they had suffered so much for. That's life.

Competition, like life, is a gift. As a team, we were living our best life.

We pulled into our training complex on campus roughly six hours after we left St. Louis at 1:00 p.m. The cheerleaders, media, some co-workers, and friends greeted us. The team grabbed their bags and headed to their vehicles to go back to their apartments. It was Sunday, and classes would begin on Monday. Training for next year would start the following week. It was a dose of reality.

Rinse and repeat. The life that produces champions is based on consistency, and the principles of success are applied when no one is watching—the simple choices made over time will be reflected in the grandest moments.

I told the team I loved them as I often did and grabbed the first-place team trophy, which sat on the passenger seat next to me on my twenty-minute ride home. The sun shone on that beautiful day.

As I pulled onto my driveway, I noticed there wasn't white snow in the yard, as there had been when I'd left for the NCAA tournament. I was gone for a total of five days. A new season was beginning. The green grass of the spring appeared.

I walked into the house and placed the trophy on the kitchen table. My dogs greeted me at the door. Their consistency to love is unmatched. They needed to go out. When I opened the back door, they stayed. Though the winter snow had melted, they wouldn't walk out onto the grass. I quickly figured out why. Shutting the door, I changed from my dress clothes to boots and sweats. Two dogs eat a ton during an Ohio winter. I re-opened the back door, walked onto the grass, and began the clean-up.

A few neighbors decorated our house with congratulatory signs on the lawn and balloons taped to the front door. My wife and children were en route home from the championship, so I was alone with my thoughts and the peace and quiet of an empty house.

I saw the trophy on the kitchen counter from the back yard. It brought me happiness, but not total fulfillment. While it reflected a job well done, it didn't offer the inner peace that could sustain me for a lifetime. I chuckled when I realized this moment was quite the opposite experience of the night before. I reflected on the weekend and my life from the hoisting of the National Championship trophy in front of thousands to the lonely clean-up in the yard.

I spent time in the space where we all spend the most time—the space between our ears. Life's temptations pull at us and never stop. Thirteen hours separated these two events. Life is funny that way—dramatically different experiences separated by hours, sometimes just minutes, and even side-by-side.

For some, it's the marriage of one's only daughter coinciding with the cancer-ridden body of a loved one. Perhaps it's the promotion at work alongside a crumbling marriage. Sometimes, things that bring happiness and disappointment happen simultaneously, and we're left to juggle it all. We're left to fill the empty space. Trophies, drugs, sex, power, money, success, and any otherworldly thing can't fill the space that we all have. It never will. Only God can sustain us in the hoisting moments of happiness as well as the heavy lifting ones.

Through death, I realized that joy is the stabilizer of this life. Joy allows us to find contentment during the chaos. As we pursue it with relentless focus, contentment is our challenge. There's serenity in the middle of chasing excellence. We must fight for both. It's the belief that regardless of what life hurls onto our train tracks, we have a higher sense of purpose, grounded by something more powerful than what this world declares.

This revelation occurred to me ten years earlier during my intensive search for the deeper meaning of life. That search, initiated by Teague's death, introduced me to the redeeming shock factor of deep suffering.

I filled two garbage bags and completed the yard work. The dogs finally felt safe enough to run out and play. I felt at peace. Our team's love for each other triumphed.

BECOMING ELITE: DATE:

1. What accomplishment are you most proud of and why?

2. How would you define happiness?

3. What are some of the side-by-side experiences you have had to manage?

4. What guidelines do you use to determine your sense of worth?

Chapter 13
Endurance

Simple over time equals substantial

*Control your thoughts. Decide about that which you will think
and concentrate upon. You are in charge of your life to the
degree you take charge of your thoughts.*

—Earl Nightingale

D o you see yourself as the landlord of your mind? This
means you seize control of what is allowed to pene-
trate our minds. What we allow is what we tolerate
and become, but we have choices. We can evict the negative
and remove it from our minds. We can dwell on the positive
and let it grow.

Trait #5: Endurance

Endurance involves practicing the basics. Many only consider
what's most valuable in their life. What do they need to be

happy? Their questions are all option-based. Their vision is too narrow.

Some people think the basics are things like working hard, going to a good college, and surrounding yourself with good people. But I believe there's something even more basic—the hunger for truth.

We want to know the truth about *how we got here*. It's one of the most fundamental questions. This question has answers, but it amazes me to discover how many people ignore the question or gloss over it. So many start with their conclusion, then seek the evidence to support their preconceived idea. Seeking the truth and then coming to a conclusion is far more reliable. We put more thought into buying a car than this truth.

When wrestlers struggle, we return them to the basics. We look at your stance. Your foundation gives you the ability to move forward, back, and side-to-side. You start your attack by winning at the simple, little things that bring lopsided results over time.

Think about this equation: Simple over time equals substantial.

As Kyle Snyder prepared for the 2019 world team trials, my mind focused on the simplest things. The suffering was coming to an end as we were just days away from the trials. The preparation was done. His body was fit. His spirit was strong. His weight was perfect. His strength both physically and spiritually was centered. It was now about execution.

As his final practice at the Ohio Regional Olympic Training center came to an end, we worked on the same things that first and second graders would learn at a youth clinic. Keep in mind, Kyle won Olympic Gold in 2016, two World titles, and three NCAA titles. He's regarded as one of the best American wrestlers of all time, and he's only twenty-two. The basics kept flooding my brain during his last session.

Kyle Snyder winning his first NCAA Championship, March 2016, in Madison Square Garden, scoring the winning points in overtime. It was one of the greatest heavyweight wrestling matches of all time. Coach Thatcher is jumping in the air. Coach Ryan is running toward the mat.

Stance, motion, stay low, move your feet, be intentional with your hand placement, and keep taking space on him. It's the simple things done well repeatedly that separate the good from the great. The old saying, "I need to get back to the basics" is divine wisdom. It doesn't matter if you're chasing Olympic gold, building a company, or repairing a relationship—the basics are life-giving. In life, these timeless tools are listening, speaking, connecting, and being curious.

We begin with the basics when our team reports to campus. We teach them lifelong necessities that'll always be foundational to growth. Of course, they'll learn how to suffer. Elite and suffering are best friends. On top of this, we instruct them on how to become a team and how to become a better team member. We do this by giving them three basic skills.

First, we teach them how to listen. They must try to understand someone else's point of view rather than spewing out their own—this a small group activity. The sessions are run by Chet Scott and his company, called Built to Lead. In small groups, they all get to share and can't ask questions until each team member has spoken. Second, once the listening portion is complete, we teach them how to speak clearly and concisely, sharing their thoughts so that others can digest them. Finally, we teach them how to write. They write their thoughts, feelings, and what they're thinking. These three skills are so important to becoming Elite and connecting with others. Connection with people will always be an integral part of growth.

The power of common sense.

During a plane trip, a Buckeye Architectural school graduate sat next to me. He shared with me that the tool we need most to climb high is common sense. The number one math professor at UNLV told me it wasn't his math skills that led him to the top of his field. He said it was common sense and its application in all things. His current job as a soil expert was to determine the structural support needed to sustain the massive hotels along the Las Vegas strip. That's impressive work. How interesting that common sense was his most needed tool. To stop, think, and quiet the madness before we act is true wisdom.

When building relationships and connections, the key to success is to be a giver and a connector. We must love people. We'll sink without them. All boats rise with the tide. We should scrutinize the tide we're choosing to swim in.

There's power in walking with the wise, the difference-makers, and the few.

When I first left Syracuse for Iowa, Tom and Terry Brands were big names in wrestling and earned that respect. They were ferocious. That's the style I wanted to emulate.

Terry watched my work ethic over the summer in the wrestling room. Eventually, we became friends and then roommates for the next three years. Though his twin brother, Tom, also wrestled, they couldn't live together because they were too competitive. Tom lived across the hall from Terry.

Living with Terry was one of the smartest decisions of my life. Not only was he disciplined in wrestling, but Terry was also clean, organized, and never drank a sip of alcohol. He was an absolute animal regarding his work ethic. Terry had the mentality I needed. He pushed me to be better. He planned to be an Olympic champion.

Eventually, Terry became a two-time World Champion and won the bronze medal at the 2000 Summer Olympics. He's now the associate head wrestling coach at The University of Iowa. His twin brother, Tom Brands, the University of Iowa wrestling head coach, won a gold medal at the 1996 Summer Olympics. Both Terry and Tom were critically important to my development as a competitor. They made a huge difference in my success and growth.

In his book *Can't Hurt Me*, David Goggins recalls his struggle to become a Navy Seal and later, an ultra-runner. Goggins relates, "When it comes to endurance sports like ultra-running, everyone can achieve feats they once thought impossible. In order to do that we must change our minds, be willing to scrap our identity, and make the extra effort to always find more in order to become more."[11]

Mindset training is huge. We teach our athletes that the winning is less controllable than your effort. Control what you can. Our effort should deplete us and bring us intense discomfort. We are capable of so much more than we think we are. You have opportunities to grow every day. We call this being the landlord of your mind.

When I trained at Iowa, I got beat badly my first day and struggled for quite a while. But each day brought a positive, which is what I focused on. My choice each day was to find small wins in each training session, such as getting a takedown one day. Another day I grabbed my opponent's leg three times. Mindset training grasps onto the small victories and growths at each practice.

A small, but difficult victory for me was to physically exert the amount of energy necessary to fight off an attacking opponent during a two-hour workout. This took an incredible amount of suffering. Because I loved it, the suffering was possible day in and day out. My body ached and life revolved around practice time, but it didn't matter. There was no place I would rather be. Though I loved Coach Gable, the Iowa program, and my teammates, I did it for me. Doing things for others isn't sustainable over time. It's a bonus, noble, and a great reason but it cannot be the foundation of excellence.

What stories play in your head? Who do you allow to rent space in your mind? As the landlord of your mind, you control these conversations and spaces. If something is negative, throw it out. Evict the minutia that consumes your thinking. You decide if you want the challenges ahead or if you want the easy way out. It's human nature to fall back into complacency, to find the easy way out. But that isn't the way of the Elite.

As a wrestler, you have to define your priceless—that objective or goal you'll do anything to achieve. My first priceless was wrestling for Iowa and winning the Nationals. Your priceless will change throughout life. I also believe you can have more than one, kind of like train tracks running parallel. When Teague died, my ultimate priceless became my faith in Jesus Christ.

Do you long for your priceless? Have you defined it? Until a wrestler answers this question, he can't become Elite. But once you do, you desire success and are willing to pay the price through chosen suffering to become Elite. Actions speak louder than words. Too often, we say we want success, but when the struggle becomes more than we imagined, we give up. An Elite athlete says, "I want to face the toughest competition. I'm ready for the toughest workouts."

Connecting your mindset to your priceless gives you the mental advantage. As the landlord of your mind, you choose the associations and influences that speak life and truth. You willingly have tough conversations because they result in growth. An active growth mindset doesn't shrink back from the truth. It continually assesses personal habits, behaviors, and thoughts to root out the harmful and replace them with life-giving ones.

Our role as coaches is to teach our athletes to be aware of what they're eating, what time they go to bed, who they spend the most time with, and what they allow to influence their minds. When they're training, I want their full attention and dedication.

One way we do this is through visualization. God says where there is no vision, the people perish.[12] Therefore, a fundamental connection piece is seeing where you want to go and perform at that highest level. Visualization allows you to imagine your priceless as accomplished.

Just as importantly, when they leave the training room, I want them to disconnect and be a normal student. I must teach an athlete how to release the stress. Using visualization techniques allows the athlete to maintain calm under pressure. Being able to shift away from duress or stress mentally plays into their success on the mat.

Kyle Snyder, Olympic champion, powerfully exhibits this mindset. Because Kyle wrestles in the heavyweight class, some of his opponents outweigh him by sixty pounds or more. I love watching Kyle wrestle. When faced with this lopsided weight competition, Kyle uses his mind. He patiently waits for angles instead of relying on strength alone. As a landlord of his mind, he evicts negative emotions that distract him and focuses instead on using his opponent's weight against him to gain the advantage.

Becoming the landlord of your mind is a lifelong process. But to be Elite, you must choose your roadmap, visualize it, and set your sights on the goal. This process is not a quick fix. It requires endurance.

BECOMING ELITE: DATE:

1. What are you tolerating that needs to be removed?

2. Have you connected your mindset to your priceless?
   Why or why not?

3. Describe your roadmap to your goal.

4. Are you willing to endure suffering if it means
   achieving your priceless?

CHAPTER 14
UNWASTED SUFFERING

Pain can wake us up to
the true priceless

We must all suffer from one of two pains:
the pain of discipline or the pain of regret.
The difference is discipline weighs ounces
while regret weighs tons.

—Jim Rohn

I can't recall loving anything more than I loved Teague. He brought all of us so much laughter. So did my two older sons, Jordan and Jake, and their younger sister, Mackenzie. Born December 1, 1998, Teague was the glue between all of my children. He loved his siblings. I would've gladly traded my life for his, but that wasn't how this journey played out.

He had a big personality and loved to compete too. He hated losing, and his favorite game was UNO™. Anyone who came over to visit had to play some UNO™. If by some chance, he was losing, he'd cheat. He didn't care. He often practiced how fast he could flip a card and say UNO™. In this game, timing mattered.

Teague mattered to me and everyone he knew. That's why I'm committed never to waste the pain of losing him. He woke me up to my true priceless.

In the summer of 2003, four-year-old Teague had his first one-on-one technique session with me. It was a beautiful morning. The sun came up early. I can remember the perfect smell of the flowers which bloomed all over the property. We lived in a small house with a great piece of land—a private acre. The outline of the property was 400 feet deep and 100 feet across. It was lined with towering pines and all sorts of flowers that bloomed most of the summer. We enjoyed the privacy so much I was willing to extend my commute to work to have it.

The house sat toward the front third of the property, which gave us a nice, grassy backyard. We often played kickball, soccer, jumped on the trampoline, or climbed the rope tied high onto a limb in the biggest tree. At the back edge of the property was the barn, and in it laid a perfect size wrestling mat for two people to improve on. Everything in the yard was put there intentionally. It was designed to have fun while building lower body and upper body power without even realizing it.

Anyone of the kids' friends who climbed to the top of the rope got an ice cream cone. There was one caveat to the guidelines. If one of the kids' friends couldn't make it to the top, one of my kids earned the ice cream for them. I loved it when the kids had friends over, particularly those who liked ice cream and were bad rope climbers. My kids always made sure everyone left with ice cream. I liked when everyone left happy.

Teague's first technique session was under his guidelines, not mine.

He walked out to the barn in the back of the yard in his underwear. He didn't have socks, shoes, or a shirt on. He didn't care. He was the king of his domain.

Jake and I were wrestling in the barn. Years later Jake would earn all Big Ten honors as a freshman wrestler for Ohio State. Teague came outside to check things out. Life didn't get any better than this. Teaching the sport of wrestling to my boys was special.

Teague wanted to join in on the learning, so I asked Jake to take off his wrestling shoes and give them to Teague. He did. Teague slid them on and laced them up. I noticed they were a few sizes too big and on the wrong

Tom teaching wrestling to 4-year-old Teague in his first-ever technique session. Summer 2002.

feet. I let him know that he put his shoes on wrong. He didn't care and didn't want to make the correction. I recommended he should take the time to put the shoes on right. He said, "No." At four years old, he was stubborn. I loved that about him. Teague stood firm in his beliefs.

Rather than force him to change, I started to teach him. I was concerned if I forced him to switch the shoes, he'd get mad and lose interest in wrestling. I allowed his *will* to prevail. I was more focused on spending some fun time together than the perfect fit of his shoes. My focus wasn't to win an argument. It was to teach him some wrestling. I wanted to make sure his first experience was a memorable one. Sure, the little things matter, but the bigger things matter more.

I worked with him on the basics. The fundamentals of a solid stance when being pulled on and pushed was important. Wrestling can be violent. So can life. The brain has to create super highways to the muscles, so when they're told to move, they do. I knew the possible advancements for Teague in the sport if he fell in love with the hard work now.

I created a fun situation between us by making it a game. We counted to five from a proper skills standpoint. Every time Teague did what was asked, he earned a point. Every time he didn't do the skill properly, he didn't get a point. Everybody likes a challenge. And everybody likes feedback. Feedback is critical—instant feedback matters.

Teague had fun, and so did I. At the end of the fifteen-minute session, I asked Jake to run in and ask his mother to come out with her camera. I wanted Teague to have a photo of his first-ever technique session.

He was going to do big things with his life. I was going to be there to pick him up when he fell because I love my kids. My wife came out, lifted her camera, and asked Teague to smile. He did that and more. As she took the photo, he raised his arms to the sky. She caught the perfect picture, one which would be with us forever.

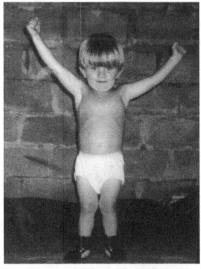

Teague's winning pose after his first wrestling session with Tom. Summer 2002

I learned that raising our arms means far more than celebrating a glorious moment.

I desired to build simple habits in him that he'd build his life on. Perhaps he'd apply these habits to a sport that could teach him so much about this life and suffering.

154

I know the way to being Elite in any endeavor is through enormous chosen suffering—a level of intense work that comes from the depth of a man's soul and a level of constant discomfort that must have a deeper purpose in our life.

For me, that deeper purpose had many prongs. The most powerful one is love. The greatest example of love was reflected by our Savior, Jesus Christ. He was slaughtered so we might have freedom and learn a better way.

I've coached men who suffer out of the love of competition, the desire to win, or the fear of being average. Others wrestle because they need to punish themselves or enjoy the emotional response to deep fatigue and the satisfaction of doing something others won't. There are so many underlying reasons and purposes for why we choose to suffer. However, none guide us as powerfully as deep love.

Finding what we love helps us build habits, focus on solutions, build an Elite mindset, and transform those around us. Find love, my friends. Know your beliefs and connect your actions to them. Write them down and fight for them. Choose the hard way. Turn a bad habit into a good one. Pursue people who lift you and move toward environments that challenge you.

1. Who or what helped you define your priceless?

2. What brings a smile to your face despite the challenges it could bring?

3. Why do you suffer?

4. Can you grasp the joy in the struggle?

5. List three people you will pursue who challenge you to be Elite.

6. Will you choose suffering to help you become Elite?

CHAPTER 15
BECOMING ELITE

Pain is a refiner and re-definer

Model the way, embrace pain and suffering,
embody truth in love.

—Chet Scott

Chosen suffering is something I witness time and again in the life of every student-athlete that masters the craft of wrestling. I also witness it in every person who is at the top of their craft and every person who lives their best life. It's embedded in the fabric of the best lived life. Chosen suffering brings us to a heightened state of awareness where extreme focus occurs. When this occurs, progress happens at an elevated rate.

We are filled with substance despite the burdens that come with this suffering. We choose whether to run toward it or away. We either look forward to causing it, or it's not even on our radar. Hard work always matters. Chosen suffering is the best friend of those who climb high. Our ability to deplete ourselves to become more is so fundamental in the journey to living our best life.

We are all on a journey to become more than we currently are. As a guide, chosen suffering delivers. It leads you toward people who think in a similar way, build your mindset, and protect it as well. Chosen suffering is a prerequisite to becoming Elite. We suffer for what we love the most. When we find it, our priceless, everyone in our lives recognizes it. There are few things more noticeable than a life lived with and for a purpose.

Stretching out of our comfort zone is always a prerequisite for growth. There are traits and choices we make. Some are timeless and good—others aren't. We must understand these principles and apply them.

Early on in my life, I understood the value in chosen suffering as it related to the sport of wrestling. This, of course, refers to the positive choices we make that stretch us.

There are also poor choices we make that cause us to grow. Poor choice after poor choice leads us closer to the bottom, which hopefully jolts us and causes a more-in-depth introspection. This pain at the bottom catapults us to hunger for something different and far greater. It is a something that lies outside ourselves.

Often, surrendering to something greater is a foundational step in the process of transforming. This transformation starts first in our mind, trusting certain principles so we can live our best life. This won't be a better life than anyone else, but *our* best life.

In 2004, it was unchosen suffering that led me to a more-in-depth inspection of my life and its purpose. For me, my chosen suffering never led me to a place of longing for the meaning of life. I missed Teague. I hurt for myself, along with his siblings and my wife. He meant so much to us.

The deep pain of losing my son, Teague, caused me to search for truth. The skeptics would say that I only looked at the facts that provided the comfort I needed, which is untrue.

Others might say I looked for a warm landing pad for a deeply saddened heart. This isn't true either.

I searched for facts. There were two options. One was that God doesn't exist. The other was that He does. That was the journey that suffering carried me along. In the end, there was simply too much evidence that pointed toward God. I lived without God, and now with Him. I find life much more enjoyable with Him.

Not everyone will go through the loss of a child. For some, it's the painful loss of a parent or loved one. For others, perhaps, it's an abusive home life, a battle with addiction, or the tragic loss of a loved one due to the mechanical failure of a vehicle or the malfunction of some other mechanical system. Maybe it's pain caused by the disloyalty of someone you trusted.

There are many scenarios this life will bring that result in deep pain. Sometimes, it's a choice we made. Sometimes, it's something way outside of our control. Regardless, it's suffering that galvanizes us and transforms us, if we willingly look at our lives outside our current circumstance. We can overcome anything. In essence, it's not so much about the suffering, but how we handle it. Be the one that overcomes it, that transforms their situation. Be the one willing to suffer, fight, and apply timeless principles to arm yourself. May the good Lord guide your steps as you chase your best you.

> YOUR WORD IS A LAMP FOR MY FEET, A LIGHT ON MY PATH.
> PSALM 119:105 NIV

There are many reasons why we're willing to choose to suffer. The grandest is love. I'd suffer for my kids because I love them deeply. We all have our motivations for why we choose to suffer.

Dick Hoyt suffered because it made his son feel like he wasn't handicapped. Dick went from not being able to finish a 3K pushing his son in his wheelchair, to finishing marathon after marathon and Ironman after Ironman in mind-blowing times. His suffering focused on his love for another. When asked to run without pushing his son because his times were so fast, he replied, "I don't run for me."

We must first realize the beauty of life in our minds. The thoughts we have matter. We should be kind and happy for others and show gratitude. We should focus on lifting rather than tearing down. It's not complicated, but we must fight the world's grip to keep a positive attitude. We grow one small step at a time. We make one simple decision to change one thing about us. Win that battle day after day, and then move on to the next one.

There's proof that God is real and readily available to anyone approaching this with an open mind. It was only under the deepest heartache that I was able to quiet the world enough to search. Learning about how God thinks reinforces the virtuous life that leads to our best life. This is a non-negotiable truth.

The world wants to trick us. It tells us to stay comfortable and avoid discomfort and pain. It tells us to take, keep busy, avoid going deep, and protect. But we can't do that if we want to live our best lives. Pains will come, and we're able to deal with it.

Becoming Elite is about letting go of the things that hold us back and pressing on. Elite begins with putting our minds in the right place. We center our thoughts to understand better the rules with which we play during our time on earth. Elite begins with developing a mindset that values the right things.

Since losing Teague, I've progressed to an even more fruitful life. Of course, there are times when I miss him terribly, but they've become more spaced out. In the meantime, I focus on serving others and finding ways to keep stretching my comfort zone.

In every stage of life, complacency longs to sneak in. We must fight this natural desire to be easy on ourselves. We should be hard on ourselves, but never down on ourselves. We must surround ourselves with people who challenge us.

Last summer, for my fiftieth birthday, I rode in the French Alps with a good friend, John Bardis. The friends I bike with locally—Chet Scott, Dave Chambers, Mike Matrka, Tom Wright, and Brett Linse—challenged me as they've done this ride together every five years. It was hot, difficult, and breathtakingly beautiful. It hurt and felt so good. We did it together, which made it better. We biked across the Italian countryside and passed through small towns that have existed for hundreds of years. John understands suffering and the great effects it creates in our lives. John's a high achiever and Elite in his field. He practices the same principles this book has shared. He also loves God, and his virtues reflect it.

Chosen Suffering. The summit of the mountain. John Bardis and me, summer 2019. My 50th birthday present.

We choose to suffer for what we love, for what we consider our identity. There is one type that lasts and fulfills, a true love. Finding what we love to do will make suffering easy. Fight for this truth.

Despite being thirteen years older than I, John powered through the 450 miles of mountain roads. It was absolutely glorious and thrilling. Every day brought a new challenge. John and I have the same birthday, and we wanted my fiftieth to be suffering-filled. You're only one decision away from chosen suffering. Start tomorrow doing something you've wanted to do but have put off.

Chosen suffering is the way. It develops many of the habits we need to become our best version. Of course, finding what we love to do won't make suffering seem so much like suffering.

I pray you take something from this book that challenges you to be your best you. Like me, you can overcome any suffering that you or living in a fallen world has caused. Sixteen years has passed since my unchosen suffering. I have moved from a terribly dark time to a place of absolute beauty. I followed principles, taking one small step at a time. You can too.

We are built for glorious things and made to stretch ourselves. We will always need to choose suffering because it's healing. We have a soul that longs to be challenged and lifted.

Choosing the hard way shows up in the little things and the big ones. It pops up on Saturday night when you have to fight your friend for the keys when she wants to drive. It shows up on a Tuesday afternoon when you have to swallow your pride and admit you were wrong. It arrives on the scene Monday morning when you don't want to get out of bed.

Regardless of the hand we are dealt, we are called to strive for more, no matter your profession or your place in life. Chosen suffering is our guide. Do hard things. Start with simple things—one at a time.

Be bold. Be strong. Be the best you, chase the truth, and keep suffering by your side. It just might become the greatest asset on your journey toward becoming Elite.

ACKNOWLEDGMENTS

The inspiration behind this book is the short but meaningful life of my five-year-old son, Teague, who left us way too soon. We loved him deeply and carry him with us in all that we do. His life helped to transform me and will impact others through the transformation he made in our entire family.

To my three children on earth who inspire me daily, Jordan, Jake, and Mackenzie, all live with purpose and have battled through their pain along with navigating the hurt they witnessed their parents deal with. Special thanks to Jake for his love and knowledge in the e-commerce space that helped get this book into the hands of those it can help grow. And for Jordan for the honest feedback on the manuscript.

To my wife, Lyn, thank you for the four amazing children and your unending belief in me. We fought to stay together, and we're better for it. You're the rock that held this family together.

To my parents, thank you for providing a foundation in things that can't be taken from me or lost. Dad, your optimism and belief are what every young person needs. Mom and Pop Sal, your example of love and stability provided me with a great example of unity. My six siblings, Deb, Frank, Sue, Rob, Chris, and Kim, thank you for making Forest Lake Blvd. a really fun home to grow up in. Frank, you were with me in the trenches on the mat and the night my world changed.

Thanks for being so strong. Life is better with you. Kimme, your big heart is a gift.

To Nanny and PopPop, may God's love and mercy be all over you. Your unselfish grace and love touched us all in the most powerful way. A big piece of you lives in each of us.

To the many assistant coaches I have worked alongside, thanks for your commitment to me, the Hofstra, and The Ohio State programs, and the many student-athletes we serve.

To the many coaches and mentors I've had, thanks for believing in me and giving me your time. Coach Hedgecock, Coach Colombo, and Coach Peppe, you made me better with your passion for knowledge and passion for what you do.

To my childhood friends, Mike Hedgecock, Jerry Castro, and Jon Adwar, I'm grateful to you.

To my teammates, both in college and high school, thank you for your effort and support. Coach Mills, Coach Carlin, Dan Gable, Jimmy Zalesky, Lenny Zalesky, Barry Davis, and Chris Campbell, thank you for sharing your coaching wisdom with me. Duane Goldman, thank you for the opportunity to get into college coaching. Thank you to all of those who've coached alongside me.

To the men who've battled on my Hofstra teams, thank you. Eric Schmiesing and Roman Fleszar, you were the first believers at Hofstra. You led the way. So many special ones fol-lowed. The combined workload among you, lifted me, and gave me an opportunity to earn the Ohio State coaching position.

To Gene Smith, thank you for believing in me and my ability to lead the Ohio State wrestling program. Bringing the Ryan family to Columbus has greatly impacted our lives for the better. Thanks to T.J. Shelton for the administrative leadership in keeping Ohio State wrestling one of the Elite programs in the country.

To the many boosters who have become part of my family, I am deeply thankful for your love and support. You're needed and have made Ohio State wrestling among the Elite places for men to grow and lead.

To Chet Scott, thank you. Your leadership has been transformational in my life. Kary Oberbrunner, my publisher with Author Academy Elite, thanks for helping me get this book done.

To Tom Rode, thank you for always caring more about where my soul is over what place my team is in. You and Julie have touched my life, my family's life, and the many student-athletes who grow under your guidance. Excited for the future of Cross Sports.

To each of my friends who helped get this book funded, I'm grateful. You've also taught me how to be a better leader—Kevin Walsh & Connie Walsh, Jack & Deb Miller, Al & Mimi Melchiorre, Travis & Laura Ulmer, Brad & Alex Jennings.

To Melissa Ryan, Jack and Deb Miller, Wayne Catan, and all those who helped me navigate my thoughts to make this book possible, I'm grateful.

To Kirsten Samuel, I thank you for your patience and endurance in working with me while going through some painful sufferings in your own life.

To Guy Savia, Steve Dutton, and Scott Arnel, thank you for your endless friendship.

To my Lord and Savior, your chosen suffering is hard for me to fathom. I am unworthy and look forward to the day when I am in your presence.

ABOUT THE AUTHOR

Tom Ryan, the award-winning head coach of The Ohio State University's NCAA National Championship Wrestling team, knows what it means to be Elite in life and work through what he terms "Chosen Suffering," a proven method for escaping complacency and embodying greatness. When he and his wife, Lynette, suffered the sudden death of their five-year-old son, Teague, they endured their most difficult crisis in unchosen suffering to discover the lesson of two-sided joy.

During his wrestling career, Tom Ryan was a two-time NCAA Division I All-American for Iowa (second in 1991, third in 1992) as a member of the Hawkeyes' 1991 and 1992 national and Big Ten championships teams. He also was a two-time Big Ten champion in 1991 and 1992. Prior to enrolling at Iowa, Ryan wrestled at Syracuse, where he was the 1989 Eastern Intercollegiate Wrestling Association Champion.

A successful coach and speaker, Tom's passion is to transform ordinary lives into Elite champions. Tom and Lynette have four children: Jordan, Jake, Teague, and Mackenzie.

ENDNOTES

1   James Allen, As A Man Thinketh (CreateSpace Independent Publishing Platform, 2006), 17.

2   Ecclesiastes 4:12 NIV

3   W. Tozer, The Root of the Righteous (Chicago: Moody Publishers, 1955, 2006, 2015) https://www.goodreads.com/quotes/700558-it-is-doubtful-whether-god-can-bless-a-man-greatly, accessed May, 15, 2020.

4   William Revell Moody, The Life of D. L. Moody by His Son, (New York: Fleming H. Revell Company, 1900), v.

5   Joseph Campbell, The Hero with a Thousand Faces, (Novato, CA: New World Library, 2008), 152.

6   Lee Strobel, The Case for Christ (Grand Rapids: Zondervan, 1998, 2016), 154.

7   Ibid., 195.

8   John 3:16-18 NIV

9   C.S. Lewis, The Problem of Pain (Quebec: Samizdat University Press, 2016. Originally published Macmillan, 1962), 26.

10 Romans 5:7-8 NLT

11 Goggins, David. Can't Hurt Me: Master Your Mind and Defy the Odds (p. 215). Lioncrest Publishing. Kindle Edition.

12 Proverbs 29:18 KJV

Coach Ryan speaks to teams, businesses, organizations, churches, and schools. His raw, relatable,
no-nonsense style makes him a preferred speaker
on topics of leadership, excellence, and becoming
Elite. Contact him today.

Instagram:
Instagram.com/buckeye158

Facebook:
Facebook.com/buckeye158

Twitter:
Twitter.com/Buckeye158

Website:
ChosenSuffering.com

Got a story inside you?

Author Academy Elite could be the right choice for helping you write, publish, and market your book.

Discover more at:
AuthorAcademyElite.com

The Ethan Foundation for Autism

Help raise funds to help families manage the challenges of caring for their beloved children.

EthanForAutism.org

CrossSports comes alongside, provides resources, and encourages the student-athletes' and coaches' growth in Christ at The Ohio State University.

thecrossports.net

BEAT THE STREETS
NYC WRESTLING

Beat the Streets aims to make a Lifelong Impact on New York City student-athletes through the benefits and skills acquired by participating in amateur wrestling.

We believe that the sport of wrestling fosters an uncommon combination of character traits that leads to enhanced social and personal development and ultimately, to better life outcomes in the youth we serve.

To Volunteer: Info@btsny.org

Website:
btsny.org

Instagram:
@beatthestreets

Facebook:
@BeattheStreetsNYC

Twitter:
@BeattheStreets

With multiple locations through Columbus, OH, and in prisons throughout Ohio, Rock City's Mission is to make heaven full.

For more information,
visit: RockCityChurch.tv

Made in the USA
Monee, IL
18 August 2022

11888065R00115